"In loving memory of our radiant, sweet, and kind Kelsey Corinne Morand who was parted from us at the age of ten."—Wendy

SPLENDID SETTINGS

100 YEARS OF MOTTAHEDEH DESIGN

WENDY KVALHEIM

PRINCIPAL PHOTOGRAPHY BY ANTOINE BOOTZ

POINTED LEAF PRESS

I. HONORING THE LEGACY OF MOTTAHEDEH   12
THE MOTTAHEDEH LIBRARY   14
WENDY KVALHEIM: A PORTRAIT   16
AT HOME IN PRINCETON, NEW JERSEY   20
DISCOVERIES IN THE KITCHEN   52
WENDY'S COOKIES   54
BY THE SEA IN KITTERY POINT, MAINE   58

II. HISTORIC COLLECTIONS   92
MOUNT VERNON, VIRGINIA   94
THE WINTERTHUR MUSEUM, GARDEN & LIBRARY, WINTERTHUR, DELAWARE   106
HISTORIC CHARLESTON FOUNDATION, CHARLESTON, SOUTH CAROLINA   118
COLONIAL WILLIAMSBURG, WILLIAMSBURG, VIRGINIA   132

III. NOT YOUR GRANDMA'S CHINA   150
A SYMPHONY IN BLUE-AND-WHITE   152
JUXTAPOSING CLASSICISM WITH MODERNISM   166
WHEN OPULENCE MEETS MINIMALISM   178
INTENSE COLORS IN AN ART-FILLED SPACE   188
FABULOUS FLORALS IN A CHARTREUSE ROOM   194
GARDEN AND WATER HUES IN A DELIGHTFUL SETTING   200
CELEBRATING PATTERN-ON-PATTERN IN NEW YORK   208
ARTS AND CRAFTS POTTERY IN A RUSTIC HOUSE   214
EXOTIC PATTERNS IN A TROPICAL PARADISE   224
ELEGANT PORCELAINS COMPLETE AN OLD-WORLD FANTASY   232

MOTTAHEDEH PATTERNS   244
WENDY'S COOKIE RECIPES   250
ACKNOWLEDGMENTS   253
INDEX   253
CAPTIONS AND PHOTOGRAPHY CREDITS   256

I. HONORING THE LEGACY OF MOTTAHEDEH

I received a legacy from Mildred Mottahedeh, who was not a "blood" but a "spiritual" relative. Knowing her since I was a child, she was my role model for a strong, intelligent woman who owned a business. In my early adulthood, she gave me the idea to study the technical and artistic aspects of her craft, and to put my skill to practice as a freelance artist and mold maker. When I was in my mid-thirties, she was 83 years old, and looking for a buyer for her 68-year-old company. She and the board of trustees of Mottahedeh agreed to sell the company to me, my husband, and our good friends, Jeffrey and Pamela Mondschein. As Mildred, her husband Rafi, and Jeffrey have passed away, the company is now owned by the three of us with the majority owned by my husband Grant and me.

The company has represented a labor of love—the love of humanity, and the love of art and design at every point in its history. Some of the features that continue to make Mottahedeh unsurpassed in the field of decorative accessories include its vision to contribute toward the knowledge of the vast history of porcelain. The sense of integrity meant that the Mottahedehs would not compromise on authenticity or quality, and their assistance to museums to fund their educational programs. Mottahedeh works with some of the best artists, factories, and lithographers in the world today, and we are proud of the long-lasting and respectful relationships that have been developed with hundreds of retailers and interior decorators across the United States and the world.

Our first book was *From Drawing Board to Dinner Table*, written for my 10th anniversary at the helm, in which I told the story of the founding of Mottahedeh by Rafi and Mildred. The book informed readers about the history of dinnerware and decorative design, as they illustrate the development of the field of porcelain. This philosophy holds true today: "The possibilities are vast. What is practical is limited. With your eyes focused toward the distance, make a beginning. Work hard, do your homework, and when you are still not sure of the correct thing to do, be brave and do what you think is right. If you decide to lead the market, you will not know until later if you made the right decision. The enthusiasm and unflagging support and loyalty of lovers of this field will let you know if your decisions were correct."

Today, it has been more than 30 years since I have been at the helm of Mottahedeh and Company. The good news is that some of the objects you have been collecting over time, have picked up at an estate sale, or have found in your aunt's attic, will be moving from the category of "vintage"—less than 100 years old—to the category of "antique"—more than 100 years old.

Most porcelain brands are associated with the factory production that gives them their name. We are a design firm that is independent of its producers as we contract with several fine companies, mostly in Europe, predominantly in Portugal, to produce our designs. We offer our goods to interior designers, retailers, and museums. This special collaboration requires finding a way to make a beautiful classic design with modern technology, through research and development. Our intention is to retain the quality that made the original so special that it has withstood the test of time and is as appreciated today as it was centuries ago. This search is the pursuit of beauty. "Make Thy beauty to be my Food," as said in the Baha'i writings.

Mottahedeh is a small, independent company that fills a special niche in our society while many similar companies have gone by the wayside. We make decorative items and historic dinnerware because we think it is important. It represents the culture of appreciating beauty. Everyone has a conception of what is beautiful and we have a rather specific one. It focuses on the best of the past, whether it is a cultural style, a refined form or a group of colors that are blended harmoniously. In more than 90 years of development, these items can be discoverd at garage sales, in attics, and take their pride of place in many homes. These objects could be toleware, brass, silver, crystal, glass, porcelain, faience, wood, or pottery. Taken as a whole, they are quite different in style, while most have an antique origin or inspiration. They are examples of our specialty of making accurate and beautiful reproductions of classic designs, brilliant objects for everyday use.

—Wendy Kvalheim

OPPOSITE Founders Mildred and Rafi Mottahedeh were photographed in 1929 on the grounds of Evergreen Place, the Baha'i meeting center in Teaneck, New Jersey. The couple had a lifelong partnership and were members of the Baha'i faith, as well as philanthropists and avid collectors of antiques. They traveled all over the world at a time when it was an uncommon thing to do, and brought back luxury goods in many mediums, including porcelain, furniture, fabrics, toleware, coins, medallions, and works on paper.

THE MOTTAHEDEH LIBRARY

OPPOSITE The Merian dinner service is an example of Mottahedeh's meticulous interpretation of historical pieces and the process that achieves it. We begin by creating a painting to match the original. We paint rather than use photographs because the image required for color separation in computer-generated silk screen lithography must be of the highest quality. The image is then printed onto waterslide paper and sealed with shellac. At the porcelain factory, this colorful decoration sheet is dipped in water and transferred to a glossy white, fired porcelain plate, then fired again. The colors we use are printed with oxides composed of powdered stone rather than ink. When fired, the oxides fuse with the surface of the plate and become permanent. Oxides liquify at different temperatures so the challenge in a manufactured process is to get all the colors to fuse in a single firing. The industry average is eight colors on a plate, while ours range from 4 to 27, the average being 16, as in the Merian pattern. Each flower has been created for the item on which it has been placed. No two flower drawings are alike.

My earliest memories of visiting Mildred at the Mottahedeh showroom at 225 Fifth Avenue in New York was to have the requisite lunch in the rather small library there. The table sat six and there were books everywhere. Mildred and Rafi had a thirst for knowledge, and they collected out-of-print and antique books on all subjects related to any sort of collecting. There were histories of early pottery and porcelain producers, books on fashion, metals, glass, compendiums of British teapots, and all manner of interior and exterior decoration, flowers, drawings, and boats. Also, there were many catalogs from Sotheby's and Christie's with sticky notes poking out that marked the pages of items they thought of interest. I consider it one of the the best decorative arts libraries anywhere, except for the library at Winterthur and a few others. The Mottahedehs collected the books over a period of 60 years, and when we bought the company, Mildred gave it to me. We built a beautiful mahogany library in 1994, with an inlaid mahogany table that seated many people.

When I am considering a new pattern or item, I go to the library, which is now in our house, and try to find the history and learn about what is authentic as a style or a period. I also go there for ideas. You only need a couple of good ideas a year. We are not making things for fashion but for long life and meaning.

When Rafi first began his business, he took classes at the Metropolitan Museum of Art in New York. He educated himself on antiquities. He was also an accomplished businessman. Mildred and Rafi's lifelong passion was to hunt for rare porcelain items that could fill out their collection while collecting for their wholesale antiques business. This collection itself illustrated the development of the porcelain trade in the East and West. Shortly before Rafi passed away, the Mottahedehs published a book with David Howard and John Ayres called *China for the West*. It was a scholarly history of the development of porcelain in China. I was fascinated by Mildred, her life, and her vast knowledge. She loved to educate those around her. I didn't get the chance to know Rafi because he passed away shortly before my husband Grant and I came to live in New York.

After World War II, Rafi and Mildred decided to buy an apartment at the newly built United Nations Plaza in New York. Mildred was involved with the United Nations at its inception and was the first Baha'i representative there in 1948. She was a friend of former Vice President Nelson Rockefeller, their friendship fueled by their love of collecting art.

Her apartment had a wonderful view of the night sky along the East River and of the waving flags during the day. They were on the 14th floor. An added feature of their location was they could zip right out of their garage onto the FDR Drive and out of the city to Stamford, Connecticut, where they had a rural home with a large garden. Mildred loved to have lots of people around and was hostess to a great diversity of ages, occupations, and ethnicities. This was a response to her belief in the Baha'i Faith. She was interested in aiding in the progress of the world. She truly believed in the value and contributions of all people.

As the apartments were being built, Mildred and Rafi had hidden cabinets, that looked like walls, built into the space and, in these, they stored their most valued artworks. They would open a cabinet and bring out objects to illustrate a point. Many guests would recount having had a fine experience at the Mottahedehs while being shown the collection. And Mildred loved to feed people. Flowers, food, and interesting stories—it was a great combination.

WENDY KVALHEIM: A PORTRAIT

I am someone who likes to make things, whether it is porcelain shapes, decorations, food, gardens, or sculptures, and I think my children have followed suit with their own artistic and design talents. I like to watch sci-fi television because there is usually a technical problem or mystery to be solved by the main characters' ingenuity. What making things involves is transformation: a change from one state to something greater. After all, a porcelain object is just a piece of clay that has been turned to stone, with some painting on it.

I believe that making things that are beautiful and sharing them is valuable. Once my father visited us when I was working at the Johnson Atelier in the modeling and enlarging department. I showed him my own sculptures, life studies of the human form. He asked me, "Why are you doing this? For your own amusement?" It occurred to me that for him, it didn't have any worth if it was not of a social or monetary value. I think that expressing yourself is initially for your own amusement or curiosity and it can develop into something much more important.

There have been several times when I have considered moving on to a different sort of job because my work is so challenging. There are both successes and failures, and a thousand ways to lose your shirt. But I found that I could not walk away from Mottahedeh if it meant that it would cease to exist without the loving care that people with vision find valuable. I am in a privileged position not to have to support myself or my family, so work for me is a passion, not a necessity. It is fortunate that the business aspect has gone hand-in-hand with the artistic nature of our company. I am one of those people who has the ability to work with both sides of the brain. I can look at financials, spreadsheets, and customs reports and also work on decorations and colors, photography, and interiors. Of course, there are people who are better at these things than I am, and we employ them so they can contribute their skills.

When a box comes into the office with just-finished samples of a new project, I have two feelings at the same time. One is excitement to see something new and wonderful; the other is a sense of dread. We might be disappointed that it isn't good or at the very least, not what we wanted: A Christmas gift or a coal in your stocking.

We are the designers. Others are the producers. The interior decorators and retailers are the presenters. The people are the users. What makes Mottahedeh is an interesting story, a curvaceous shape, a complexity of design, brilliant colors, and an aha-moment. Mottahedeh pieces are eminently usable. They echo the past yet are meant for modern living.

What keeps it all going? We concentrate on being of service to our clients. We do our best to make it easy for them. After all, nobody really, really needs what we make. It is a question of need versus want. But for some, the beauty of one's environment is an essential need and desire.

OPPOSITE The first thing one sees when walking into our home in Princeton, New Jersey, is a scene of trees, birds, and water by the Gracie Studio, a New York-based company that specializes in hand-painted wallpapers. My portrait was taken in front of the console in the hall. The cachepot is in the Tobacco Leaf pattern. I sculpted the verdigris sculpture, *Danceflower*, first in plasticine, then cast it in bronze with the lost wax method, and finished it by welding and chasing it in bronze.

RIGHT The handsome mahogany library in our house has had several incarnations. It was first built for the Mottahedeh showroom at 225 Fifth Avenue, in New York. It was elegant and imparted a sense of gravitas to our visitors. By the time we joined the company, Mottahedeh had been in New York for more than 60 years. The building began as a hotel in 1907, later becoming doctors' and lawyers' offices. At the time the Mottahedehs moved in, it was known as the New York Gift Building, for many years the city's premier showcase for glass, ceramic, and silver giftware, before being converted into luxury apartments. In 2004, we moved into a showroom on the 21st floor at 41 Madison Avenue—the well-known tabletop building—that became our home for 18 years. The light-filled showroom was reconstructed using the casegoods from 225 Fifth Avenue, and had unobstructed views. But as there was not enough space for the gorgeous library, we moved it as a custom installation to Princeton. On the top shelf are three versions of the Monteith bowl with its indented rim. In the center, is the Kanxi period (1662-1722) blue-and-white Monteith bowl, an authorized reproduction of one in the Metropolitan Museum of Art in New York. At right, is the Reagan Monteith bowl, which was designed for Ronald and Nancy Reagan as a parting gift to his cabinet members when the president left the White House in 1983. The panel shows the "Great Seal" and the backstamp states, "Presented by the President and Mrs. Reagan: Recalling eight memorable years 1981–1989." At left, is the Millennium bowl, a limited-edition presentation bowl, which was inspired by the Reagan bowl to mark the new millennium. The center of the bowl shows a historical map of the world. We used the style of Golden Butterfly, adding the blue-and-orange moth motif of the Rockefeller reproduction dinner plate.

AT HOME IN PRINCETON, NEW JERSEY

For anyone interested in the history of the founding of our nation and the decorative arts of the last few centuries, Princeton, New Jersey is the perfect place to live. Founded in 1635, the town is steeped in lore about the Revolutionary War, including the travels back and forth of the Continental Army led by George Washington, as well as the British, who were greatly outnumbered from the outset. It is the home of Princeton University and as such, has fine theater, dance, and music; an art museum and the renowned Princeton Institute for Advanced Study. The Princeton School of Public and International Affairs has been home to many world leaders and thinkers. Presidents James Monroe and Woodrow Wilson, as well as Albert Einstein, were residents there for many years. Princeton is also a pretty town, bustling with college students, families, and small children.

My family, three children and my husband Grant, have lived here for 35 years. Our house is set way back in the woods in an area that once belonged to the founders of a number of pharmaceutical and telecommunications companies.

We moved to there when I was apprenticed at the Johnson Atelier for Sculpture in Hamilton, New Jersey, and Grant was working on Wall Street in New York. I was in the modeling and enlarging department, working on life-sized figure sculptures and making monuments, as well as my own still-life figures. Previously, I had earned a degree in sculpture from the Pratt Institute in Brooklyn, New York.

Our brick-clad saltbox is traditional in style. It has a staircase in the front foyer that leads up to the second floor and because it was unfinished when we bought the house, we called it the "staircase to nowhere" as there was no second floor. The previous owners, who had bought some plans that included a second floor, had built the house three feet too short to put it in—something we realized when we wanted to do just that. The painted pine risers and balusters were clearly temporary. But, eventually, a dark and lustrous mahogany staircase became the central focus of the foyer, and since then, we have made many other improvements, including installing teak parquet for the floors and hand-painted wallpaper from Gracie throughout the main section of the house.

Over a 35-year period, we expanded the house to accommodate more people, changing the existing two-car garage to a large room for gatherings, adding an apartment over the new garage, and an arts and crafts room in the basement-playroom.

We also gutted and redesigned the kitchen with enough space to serve a crowd—incorporating two refrigerators, two ovens, three dishwashers, and a six-burner stove. Off the kitchen, we built a large dining room to seat 14 people and added a 20-foot-long window seat.

I believe that a house should be a home that reflects your lifestyle, your tastes, and your family life. Ours has become a gathering place and a community center of sorts. While we focused on family activities, family dinners, and playing games together, we have also thought it important to welcome people we know as well as the people we didn't, and to offer an open place for discussion on the topics of the day, a home-cooked meal, and a congenial sense of hospitality. At the outset, we make it clear that we are not going to talk about partisan politics. It is a difficult balance.

Every few months, we host a large buffet dinner, a presentation, open conversation, and some nice desserts over coffee and tea. We call this the "meeting of the minds." We start it off with perspectives gleaned from the Baha'i Faith, inviting people of any faith, race, or ethnicity to join in, as the principle of the Baha'i Faith is that there is only one religion, the religion of one God, and that all races are members of the same human family. Achieving unity in our diversity is today's biggest challenge. I cook the dinner. My husband and two of our close friends set it up, serve it, and do the yeoman's job of cleaning up. On Sunday mornings, the Baha'is and their friends in the surrounding area come together with their children to talk about community and the need to acquire virtues. They sing songs, hear a story about truthfulness or courage, work on a crafts project, and run around outside using the riding toys, and draw with chalk on the driveway. Building happy memories of family time together is important in our lives, creating a circle of interest, love, and support.

A song we taught our children and grandchildren represents my hope for your home.

My home is the home of peace,
My home is the home of joy and delight,
My home is the home of laughter and exaltation.
Whosoever enters through the portals of this home, must go out with a gladsome heart.
–Baha'i writings

OPPOSITE In the living room, our limited edition Millennium bowl, with the message, "The Earth is but One Country and Mankind Its Citizens" commemorates the turn of the last century.

OVERLEAF The formal living room has been decorated in a combination of greens, rust, and black hues to complement the teak parquet floors. The Merian porcelain lamps are some of the Mottahedeh pieces in the room. The lithographs on the wall are scenes of New York City's Central Park by the New York artist Harold Altman. In spite of its formality, the living room is one of the places where we frequently host gatherings for large groups of people. I believe that even formal spaces should be used often without worrying about heavy traffic. The crystal pieces are by Moser, Murano, and Lalique. The piano was a gift to my mother from my grandmother, an accomplished pianist and voice coach. I did not inherit the musical gene and I never learned to read sheet music. *Danceflower*, the verdigris bronze sculpture is one of three I made.

LEFT The Millennium bowl is displayed on a burled mahogany coffee table in the living room.

OPPOSITE Mildred Mottahedeh said that the inspiration for the plate in our living room came to her in a dream. The words of the "Tablet of Ahmad," a special prayer known well to the Baha'is, encircles the rim. It reads, "Lo, the Nightingale of Paradise singeth upon the twigs of the Tree of Eternity, with holy and sweet melodies, proclaiming to the sincere ones the glad tidings of the nearness of God." The central symbol is a calligraphic rendering in Arabic by the calligrapher Mishkin-Qalam, whose meaning is: "O Thou the Glory of the Most Glorious!," later adopted by Baha'is everywhere: a reference to God, defined as the essence that animates the universe.

RIGHT A Mottahedeh reproduction Ch'ien Lung bowl sits on an Indian natural white marble table inlaid with semiprecious gem stones in a pietra dura design. Marble inlay, a delicate process that involves carefully cutting and engraving marble shapes by hand, is a closely protected traditional art and only a few experts are skilled enough to currently do it justice. To begin the process, a predefined pattern such as a floral geometrical design is engraved on the marble slab. Then, small pieces of precious and semiprecious stones of different shades are cut delicately and precisely to fit into the grooves: white jasper, green malachite, yellow tigereye, red jasper, blue lapiz lazuli, green aventurine, black onyx, yellow jasper, sky-blue turquoise, abalone shell, white mother-of-pearl, and red coral.

RIGHT The breakfront in the living room is a reproduction of a Chinese Chippendale design from Baker Furniture Stately Homes Collection; the love seat is from Baker Furniture and the side tables are from Baker furniture Historic Charleston Collection. In the breakfront, the three most notable antiques are the original Ch'ien Lung bowl, *middle left*, made for the Chinese emperor in 1735 and a rare example of white-on-white, captured in six-petalled flowers on a blue background; the cobalt blue decorated Ming plate, *middle right*, that dates from the Yongle period, was in the Mottahedehs' collection. I bought it later at a Sotheby's auction on September 20th, 2000, as a birthday gift to my husband, Grant. The Merian dessert plate, *middle center*, dates from about 1735. Mildred Mottahedeh was not a blood relative of mine, but was like my great aunt. One day she asked me to draw a nine-pointed star for the center of a Ming plate, called Palace Blue, a design at the Metropolitan Museum of Art in New York. This might sound easy, but I was daunted by the subject and especially by the museum. Today, you can just Google for an array of design solutions, but there was no internet then. Online references about porcelain design are still quite thin today and the history of porcelain is found mostly in books. If you want to go deeply into the subject, take the old-fashioned way, go to a library. All I knew was that the plate was a blue Ming design. I went to the Metropolitan Museum to look at Ming. It was surprisingly simple, yet complex. The line work was fluid yet precise, in melted cobalt blue, belying years of effort to achieve the perfect effect. It was humbling. These centuries-old ceramics had endured. But what was Ming? To make something with the style and appearance of a known work of art, you need to understand the artist's place and time. So began my desire to unlock the mystery of creative people who were creators in their own day.

OPPOSITE AND RIGHT The Merian pattern is the first I worked on when I came to Mottahedeh in 1992 and is dear to my heart for many reasons. It is one of the most complex patterns we make. Merian shares a space alongside Tobacco Leaf, for its number of colors and delicacy of design. It features raised colorful enamels with gold accents and beautifully detailed butterflies and flowers inspired by the drawings of 17th century botanical illustrator and scientist, Maria Sybilla Merian. The original plate, *opposite*, which was the genesis of the Merian pattern, was a Chinese porcelain dessert plate, from about 1735, which was in Mildred and Rafi Mottahedeh's collection. The dessert plates include four center motifs, of which the iris is the original design.

RIGHT In the current version of the Merian pattern, there are 25 separate silk screens as well as raised enamels all baked in the kiln at the same time. As with any design we prepare to offer, we think about the sensibilities and uses of today, so the Merian plates can go in the dishwasher. The original still lifes of the pattern included chewing and flying insects, and the flowers had holes in the petals. For the dinner and bread plates, we turned a caterpillar into a leaf and only have flying insects and pretty bugs.

LEFT A hand-crafted brass chandelier that Mottahedeh produced in India in the 1990s in a limited edition hangs in the formal dining room. The mahogany table is set with Merian dinnerware and serving pieces. The crystal stemware is in the Montaigne Optic pattern from Baccarat. The porcelain in the cabinet includes our Palace Blue tea service, licensed by the Metropolitan Museum of New York and a blue-and-white covered meat platter. The silver is a collection of various English tea services. Other silver pieces include a candelabrum from Georg Jensen made by Alphonse LaPaglia in 1940, called Spring Glory.

OPPOSITE The china, in the Merian pattern, has been set on placemats we designed and that were hand-sewn in Madeira by Sharyn Blond. I felt that the Trianon silverware with its braided vine motif from Odiot, perfectly matched the porcelain's intertwining blue and orange chain border. The hand-hammered silver water pitcher is from Buccellati.

PREVIOUS PAGES A series of pieces in Mottahedeh's Famille Verte pattern are displayed on the inlaid mahogany sideboard, a Hickory Chair Furniture Company reproduction of a Hepplewhite design. The chairs are Chippendale reproductions from Councill. The crystal stemware is in the Montaigne Optic pattern from Baccarat. The tall vase is a vintage Mottahedeh piece that we found in our rare room—a collection of one of everything we made for about 80 years—and fell in love with it. The porcelain vegetables were hand-made by the Boston, Massachusetts–based artist Katherine Houston.

LEFT AND OPPOSITE The understanding of porcelain colors and firing over centuries was developed in China, long before it was known in Europe. This was a well-kept secret that allowed a huge trade to develop with the West. Europe was wild for porcelain. The first glazes consisted of celadon, a light grey-green made with copper. The most stable and earliest glazes were made with metallic oxides—iron for red and copper for green, as well as cobalt for navy blue. Famille Verte pieces use iron red and copper green, which gives them their name: Green Family. The Famille Verte pattern, predominantly made by Vista Alegre, adorns more than 45 different items and is sold in their shops in Portugal. For a few years, we partnered with Sharyn Blond Linens to make delightfully hand-embroidered placemats and napkins in Madeira, Portugal. We made a number of styles to go with our dinnerware, including grey and red napkins for Famille Verte, but we found that it was difficult for a porcelain company to move into linen sales, so we gave up that dream.

PREVIOUS PAGES With beautiful plates, all I usually need on the table are flowers, accented by glassware in complementary colors, and a beautiful tablecloth. The use of rose, red, and purple with the Ch'ing Garden pattern provides a dramatic effect. Keeping the flowers low allows guests to talk to each other easily and the flowers, not their containers, become the focus. The goblets, by Varga Art Crystal, were available from Mottahedeh in the 1990s. The silver and gold flatware is from Alain Saint-Joanis.

LEFT AND OPPOSITE For Ch'ing Garden, I combed through our library of books and settled on a Chinese Export plate that had several elements that could be transposed. We needed a basket motif for the elegant hanging flowers. I thought that a wicker border would go nicely, and the abundant and delicate tree leaves would fill the shoulder of the plate. The line work of geometric shapes and stylized flower baskets, *opposite*, would be etched using gold to give the design sparkle. The background of the Colonial Williamsburg, in Williamsburg, Virginia, wallpaper that was used as inspiration was in a yellow tone that I felt the pattern needed. The genius of the design is the violet accents that were in the original wallpaper. The basket of flowers motifs are taken from an original wallpaper at Colonial Williamsburg. There were only three baskets in the wallpaper and we needed one more for our set of four dessert plates so we designed one of our own.

LEFT AND OPPOSITE The ceramic tile wall mural and Kohler water fowl sink in the powder room were spin-offs from Colonial Williamsburg's Ch'ing Garden dinner service, inspired by the Chinese wallpaper at Colonial Williamsburg. Both the mural and the sink were Mottahedeh designs created for Kohler. The sink motifs were derived from Audubon life studies and colored to match the wall mural. The bespoke carved wood chair was made by Colin Almack of Beaver Furniture, a woodworking studio in Yorkshire, England. A little beaver has been carved on every piece of furniture as the trademark of the company that specializes in cool-aged oak. We ordered this chair while we were on our honeymoon in 1979, and received a matched set of furniture the following year. A trio of stylized Yorkshire roses have been carved on the back of the chair.

OPPOSITE Chelsea Feather is an updated and simplified version of a plate shape we have carried for many years. The shape is a replica produced at the Chelsea Manufactory, one the earliest English factories, which was established around 1740 and operated until 1745, when it merged with another ceramics producer. Chelsea is known for its animals, figurines, and botanical shapes, done in an elaborate painting style. The three patterns we have made in this shape are Chelsea Botanicals, Duke of Gloucester, and Chelsea Bird. Chelsea Feather Gold is versatile and elegant. We have also developed Chelsea Feather Turquoise. On a red tablecloth with gold overprinting, and vermeil flatware, it creates a dramatic table setting. The rose-colored handcut stemmed goblet is a design we created with Varga Art Crystal in Hungary, but is no longer available. The small fish tureen, hand-painted in coral and gold, is a reproduction by Vista Alegre, from the National Museum of Ancient Art in Lisbon, Portugal.

RIGHT For the gold feathering along the edge of the rim, we took our cue from the decoration of the Duke of Gloucester pattern—22-karat matte gold. Matte gold fires at a lower temperature than the other colors as it is a soft metal, so it is best to avoid putting the pieces in the dishwasher at a high heat. A delicate wash cycle and air-drying are recommended.

LEFT AND OPPOSITE It is known from excavations of the grounds at Mount Vernon, Virginia, that George Washington, America's first president, used this dinner service at home. The version that existed at the time was a very durable Staffordshire salt-glazed stoneware with a grey-white body. The Prosperity dinner service Mottahedeh created replicates the fine, reticulated surface of the plates but was captured with scanning and 3-D printing, and produced in thin, bright white, high-fire porcelain. The rim of the plate is unglazed, and the service is stain-proof and dishwasher and microwave safe. If ever something historical can be improved upon, this is it. The tureen can be used for many a feast and cleaned in the dishwasher. That's what I call modern. While you may have seen tureens of this kind of English Staffordshire salt glaze, this is one you have not seen as it was composed of thin porcelain, with some parts glazed and some parts unglazed, and didn't exist before. Our secret is that we took a number of elements from five different tureens we liked and fashioned a new, improved, and graceful historical tureen. We hope you will find it as lovely as we do.

OVERLEAF We thought that serving tea for two was a very fine idea, which inspired the Lace Tea for Two set of cups, saucers, and a sugar bowl that stack up neatly. This set is decorated in the Cornflower Lace pattern with a banding of gold and is also available in Cobalt Blue, Leaf Green, and Apple Green.

OPPOSITE Mottahedeh has partnered with Rookwood Art Pottery to introduce vintage and classic vessels that reflect the rich history of Rookwood, one of America's most honored decorative arts companies. Founded in Cincinnati, Ohio, in 1880 by Maria Longworth Nichols, Rookwood Pottery was the first female-owned manufacturing company in the United States. In our oak dining room, a more casual space we added in 1998, the lithograph above the vintage Stickley sideboard was created by Graciela Rodo Boulanger, a Bolivian artist, whose work depicts stylized children and animals, musical instruments, and sports. In 2015, I developed, with Rookwood Pottery, a series of pieces that include a brown stoneware lamp and two footed bowls that were named Orion, for Orion's belt, and were inspired by early designs of American art pottery. I produced these in 2015 with the Rookwood Pottery now operating in its hometown in Cincinnati.

RIGHT The dining table was custom-made by Stickley to seat 14 people. The tabletop is made of one solid piece of oak and is so heavy we couldn't move it if we tried. The dinnerware is part of Mottahedeh's Milestone series that debuted in 2000—fine stoneware at a lower price point that is simpler in style than our traditional patterns. Called Leaf and shown here in Blue Haze, it was inspired by studying Korean and Chinese glazes and the outline of a leaf that had been fused onto a black plate in the style of raku. The bamboo placemats were handmade in Myanmar and the bamboo-handled flatware is by Alain Saint-Joanis, in France.

DISCOVERIES IN THE KITCHEN

Cooking is a lot like the plastic arts—painting and sculpture—with some chemistry thrown in. At the same time, making ceramics like porcelain is sort of like making a cake. You stir up a mixture, pour or form it into a shape, bake it until solid, and then decorate it or not. Since much of the beautiful porcelain we are familiar with is paired with food, we appreciate it most often at the dinner table.

As a child, I spent hours in the kitchen. Though my mother did not really like to cook, she never missed an opportunity to encourage her children to explore anything that could develop creativity. Efficiency was paramount to her. The only cakes she made were from a box and we did not have dessert as part of a meal. She was very interested in the health benefits of good nutrition and whole foods and often brought my two brothers and me articles or books on the subject. We frequently had guests for dinner, either on an impromptu basis or by invitation far in advance. These guests ranged in age, color, ethnic backgrounds, and economic standing and were extremely interesting. Dinner was never elaborate or visually elegant, but there was always enough food, no matter who showed up. We were encouraged to taste everything, familiar or not. I loved to sit at the dinner table. Meals were at 6:00 pm sharp and all who were home were required to attend. The discussion was about books read or philosophical questions. These meals provided me with a foundation of good conversational ability and an ongoing curiosity about different points of view.

For me, cooking and baking were forms of recreation. It was relaxing to be in the kitchen and the activities offered endless answers to questions. What happened when you put cornstarch into a pot with hot water? What happened when you put it in cold water and heated it? What was the secret to cake frosting that it would stay on a cake? How do you make different colors? What tastes good? What tastes bad? What happens when the same recipe is cooked at different temperatures? How much is too much of something? How much is too little?

Not only did my mother allow me to go into the kitchen to experiment, she usually did not expect me to clean up. What a gift this was and what patience it required on her part. Children rarely tire of doing things over and over again unless they are made to feel uncomfortable by doing something incorrectly, and their actions are fueled by endless curiosity. Their capacity to learn so quickly is greatly facilitated by their ability to keep on trying to figure things out, even if it takes them 200 tries. They will watch an animated film seven times, if it's one they like. Time is not a consideration. They can be very focused, having minds that absorb any and all information around them. They must be given quiet time and time to get bored if they are to develop their talents for discovery.

It occurred to me then that baking and cooking could make a lot of people happy. It was also a necessary part of feeding a family. One event that affected my family is that our mother contracted polio when I was six months old. In 12 grueling days, she lost the use of her legs to spinal nerve damage. All the household activities that she carried out so valiantly, such as shopping, driving us to lessons, and making meals, were physically very difficult for her to do. At about the age of nine, I began to put together meals for the family, under my mother's guidance. The biggest challenge to making a full meal is to finish cooking everything and get it on the table at the same time, whether hot, or in some cases, cold. Here again, my family was very patient, because there were many times when they ate meals in stages, depending on what was finished cooking. They would say things like: "This is great, here come the peas. When do we get the meat?" Once a cook masters the individual steps to a meal, the real sign of competence is orchestration.

Food has been a hobby of mine since those days. Good food and wonderful meals can be great enhancements to family life. Today it is possible to learn to make all kinds of dishes thanks to the great cooking shows on the Food Network, and from all the wonderful books and culinary magazines. After we introduced the first book called *From Drawing Board to Dinner Table*, which talks about the history of Mottahedeh and great porcelain masterpieces through the ages, we thought the natural next step would be to show ways to create environments that enhance great meals. We hope you enjoy them and that they help you to create your own meaningful traditions of togetherness.

OPPOSITE If you wonder where Wendy is, the first place to look is in the kitchen. The grandchildren come into the house and run down the hallway to the kitchen to see what is cooking. There is usually something abrew. Then they pull up a chair and ask to help. Here, we are making pasta with the grandchildren. It is usually messy and unpredictable, but always fun, especially if you get to eat it at the end. Their parents have sharpened their skills with lots of home projects. As you might guess, making cookies is a favorite.

WENDY'S COOKIES

It's always the right time for a cookie break! We can find any excuse for eating a cookie. I love most kinds of cookies, preferably crisp ones. Sorry, soft cookie lovers. In our family, we have many cookie bakers.

At every New York Tabletop Show, I offer a new, as well as a tried-and-true selection of cookies. More often than not, people ask me for the recipes. Not only do they look pretty on a plate, they also deliver wonderful flavors. We have very pretty patterns, so we have paired each cookie with a plate and we give the cookie recipe to go with it. In my forays into baking for the show, I was not only looking for good flavor, but also for volume. Thus, these recipes are not fancy, but easy to produce in large quantities and they also freeze well. I would make them far in advance and freeze them in airtight containers for a month or longer. All this time, my kids would come and go in the kitchen probably thinking how motherly I was by making them cookies. My husband, being a big fan of cookies, too, would require receiving what we called the "Daddy Tax"; a certain percentage would go in his mouth. He was usually offered the less perfect cookies and strenuously objected to the overcooked ones. You must make a lot of cookies to keep up with the pre-event crowd. Cookies of all variations include four things: flour, sugar, butter, and often eggs. These are the ones that have been favorites for several years. Over my baking career, I have changed some of the recipes to bring out what I like better, in chewiness or flavor. I am also heavy on the nuts and have usually increased what the recipe calls for.

One word of advice: the proportions of ingredients in baked goods are very important. It is not wise to try to change them. Cookies don't like being messed with! One point that bakers know is that moist ingredients should be mixed together separately from the dry ones—except for sugar as I throw that in with the butter. Butter, eggs, and liquids should go together first. The wet and dry ingredients should be mixed together as a final step and usually mixed together just enough to incorporate. Too much mixing can make your cookies tough.

OPPOSITE Golden Shortbread on a Blue Dragon shell dish.

OVERLEAF Top row from left, Surprisingly Minty Chocolate Sandwiches in a Blue Canton–covered rectangular box; Almond Flavor Thumbprints on a Sacred Bird & Butterfly plate; Pistachio Sablés on a Tobacco Leaf plate; Oatmeal Lace and Spice Cookie on a cornflower Blue Lace fluted tray. Bottom row from left, a Wendy's Marzipan Slice cookie on a Gabriel luncheon plate in currant; Date Walnut Bars on a Longton Hall cookie plate; Triple Nut Pecan cookies on a Chinoise Blue square tray; and a Chocolate Walnut Cherry Jumbles cookie on a Virginia Blue plate.

BY THE SEA IN KITTERY POINT, MAINE

People have many ideas about Maine. I think of the rocky coastline interspersed with sandy coves, the smell of salt breezes and pine, the hot summer days and cool summer nights, dragonflies making a frenzied dinner of mosquitos. It is an unpretentious life where little in the way of personal possessions is required, or in many cases, available. And then there is "lobsta," harvested right along the rocky coast. For me, Maine embodies my most important childhood memories with family and friends. But most of all, the steady waves and tides draw one's mind into a contemplative state, unencumbered by thoughts of the minutiae that can fill each day.

There is a spot over the New Hampshire-Maine border, three miles from Portsmouth, that was once a three-story hotel and later became a retreat called Green Acre Baha'i School, which it still there today. Growing up, we didn't go on vacations, but we went to Maine and to Green Acre.

When I was 12 years old, our grandfather bought a half-acre of land in Eliot, Maine, on which stood a little un-winterized bungalow. It had a cast iron washboard sink in the galley kitchen and he installed a bathroom to replace the outhouse. It might be comfortable for four people. We loved being there with way more than four people—cousins and other family members. Not much room to move around, but it could sleep 11 people. We didn't mind; we would burst outdoors and walk to the Piscatiqua River estuary or ride our bikes down the narrow road to the corner store.

When I was 40 years old, my husband and I had the opportunity to buy the property owned by my mother and her two sisters. "The cottage," as we called it, at this point, was completely run down so some family members called it "the shack," but I preferred "the shanty." On that spot, we built a contemporary clapboard house with four bedrooms in New England vernacular style with a Belgian-block fireplace that rose 24 feet up the center of the house. The New England neighbors raised their eyebrows and said nothing, which is their way. We saw it as a gathering place for our extended family, many members of whom lived nearby. They would take turns renting the house for a nominal fee and attend programs at Green Acre.

Our forays into Maine did not stop there. The ocean calls people, witnessed by the fact that 40 percent of the U.S. population lives in coastal counties, while the landmass is only 10 percent of the country. We saw many houses but they were sub-par. At the last moment one Columbus Day weekend, we decided to see one more house. It had been on the market for 18 months. It was a brilliant blue-sky day. We passed down a wooded, winding road and came upon a large house within 100 feet of the ocean. When we stepped into the foyer, it was as if we were on a boat, because only the sparkling ocean twinkling with thousands of points of light was visible. As we stepped closer to the living room's bay window, two classic Adirondack chairs sitting side by side came into view. Walking through the kitchen and out onto the green lawn, we went right to the chairs and sat down. That was it. We were home. The amazing thing was that the house did not need fixing up. The woodwork was painted white and the walls were a neutral mushroom color. As was the case in Princeton, when we first moved in, everything in the house, including the walls and furniture was beige or white. I spent a decade irradicating beige in Princeton. In Kittery it was possible to add color to the pieces of furniture and decorative accessories, which we did.

The East Coast shoreline offers a dream-like view of the sun rising from the sea with its shades of pink, orange, and the most brilliant blue sky. It rises fast and unless you get up early, you miss it. But on the West Coast, one gets the outstanding sunsets over the water. It makes me want to see both coasts. On a clear day, the Kittery house is flooded with light.

What is most special about the property are the abundant gardens and seasonal blooms set against the ocean, which attract family and guests to the beautiful environment. First, there are daffodils and forsythia, followed by crocus, rhododendron, and lilacs. Then come the peonies for a brief unveiling; the lilies in orange; yellow and pink azalea; giant hosta; white Shasta daisies; lavender roses; masses of multicolored hydrangea; coral bells; beach roses; dune grasses; and blueberry bushes. Finally in the fall, sedum with pink flowers that the bees love, geraniums year-round, and yellow witches' broom. I am sure there are flowers I have forgotten to mention.

PREVIOUS PAGES While there are many homes on the ocean in Maine, it is somewhat rare to find one with a manicured lawn abutting the rocky shoreline. In stormy weather, powerful waves throw 10-pound rocks onto the lawn. Almost every morning in the summer, a small tourist fishing boat carrying day visitors sidles up to the shore's edge. In the hope of catching some bass that are known to like this rocky spot, they throw in a fishing line or two. There might be a dog on the boat jumping around. They spend about an hour—them looking at us and us looking at them. Then they motor away, just like clockwork.

OPPOSITE One home becomes two. Our first house has welcomed many visitors and family members and while it is large, there are just four bedrooms. We thought of building a guest cottage on the property, but that did not come about. About ten years into our stay, the house next door came up for sale. Both properties were covered with brush and small trees, as well as tall pines. The owners of the house had tried to build a stone wall about 10 feet high to be a patio with a great ocean view. And, we had watched them build it only to see it turn into 50 tons of rubble as it didn't have the proper infrastructure. That was the biggest deterrent for them to sell the property. But we knew what it could become. We took on this project with determination and rebuilt the wall, only this time into two four-foot-high terraces. We left room for flowers and ornamental grasses and for children to walk between them. And we added garden seats. A child could now only fall four feet at a time, something which I considered a great improvement.

PREVIOUS PAGES In Kittery, a jungle of underbrush and small trees between our two houses was replaced with a lawn, which allowed us to see one house from the other. A newly exposed outcropping of rock became a garden with a pathway between the houses.

LEFT The Mottahedeh hawks on the mantelpiece are reproductions of pieces that were in the Nelson Rockefeller collection.

OPPOSITE The Wufu cachepot or flowerpot, which is filled with hydrangeas of different hues that appear around the house, is one of our patterns that is often rich with symbolism, as are the Chinese designs that adorn them. I found the inspiration for the cachepot in a Sotheby's catalog of Oriental antiquities. It was five-sided but had a straighter shape. Ours is five-sided but has lobes that make it quite curvy, and five turquoise feet, each in the symbolic shape of a bat. The surface pattern is composed of beautiful and graceful little bats from another source. While this is not a reproduction, it takes its meaning from the Wufu Bat or the Five Blessings: health, long life, prosperity, virtue, and a tranquil and natural death.

PREVIOUS PAGES Judy King, an interior designer who is also a friend and neighbor, collaborated with me on the design of the light-filled, two-story-high living room that offers a full view of ocean. The sofa echoes the round shape of the bay windows that are opened wide in the summers to allow in refreshing breezes. Blue Hot Island glass vases from Maui, Hawaii, which remind us of the swirling eddies schools of fish just below the water surface have been arranged on the Aria black walnut sideboard, from Thos. Moser in Auburn, Maine. The tiered condiment server is a vintage Mottahedeh creamware item with shell-shaped bowls. The lamp bases are faux coral. The high-backed Iribe chairs are from L. & J.G. Stickley in Manlius, New York. The blown-glass tortoise comes from Murano, Italy. Duffy Sheridan, the American artist who has been strongly influenced by the Baha'i Faith, painted the photorealistic scene of the olive trees in the Baha'i Gardens in Akko, Israel.

RIGHT The sofa was appropriately upholstered in a fabric with green seaweed motifs in reference to the seaweed-covered rocks. The rocks, as well as the wind-crested waves, made me think that we needed a green stone table. So I found stone that matched my imagination at a nearby rock quarry. It was a deep feldspar green with chunks of blue that are only visible in a certain light—like the sea—always changing yet the same. Labradorite is a member of the feldspar family. The stone is composed of aggregate layers that refract light as iridescent flashes of peacock blue, gold, and pale green. I bought a slab and had it cut to size. As people don't usually notice its colorations, it is like a secret. Mottahedeh urns, Dolphin candlesticks, and a Dolphin centerpiece sit atop the table.

PREVIOUS PAGES AND RIGHT A black walnut table called Aria, from Thos. Moser, has been set up at one end of the spacious living room with our Lace pattern—that comes in a variety of colors and can be mixed for a delicate and cheerful effect. We often set the table with this versatile pattern. Lace started off as a dinner service in cobalt blue and is now made in five colors: pink, apple green, cornflower blue, leaf green, and cobalt blue. People are sometimes worried about how to use porcelain pieces because they don't know the etiquette and are concerned about making a mistake. My point of view is there are no rules. We would not have any qualms about serving a dessert in a teacup. It is also fun to mix the colors, which is one reason we think Lace pattern is so popular. The painting over the fireplace is by Carol Rowan, an artist who divides her time between Maine and Washington, DC.

OPPOSITE Sunrise and sunset, when the shadows are long and the colors are bright, are my favorite times of the day. While in the winter, strong breezes come off the ocean continuously, summer heat calms the waves to a certain stillness. Regardless of the season, there is always a raft of grey ducks bobbing on the water close to shore.

OVERLEAF Cakes are celebratory for birthdays and for many other parties they help create memories. The Lace pattern and cakes go very well together. Large or small footed cake plates, oblong trays, and dessert plates make a spectacular display whether the cakes are fancy or plain. Flowers in our Wheatsheaf vase provide the finishing touch. Do vary the height of the plates to make the table look more interesting. And don't forget the cookies.

OPPOSITE AND RIGHT The name of this pattern is Sylvanae, which is the Latin word for goddesses of the forest. An apt name for this adaptation of a Zsolnay Porcelain Manufactory design first produced in the late 1800s in Pecs, Hungary. The swirling motif features exotic birds and multicolored flora, intertwined with leaves, on a generously sized plate. Wendy Rahn, a fine artist, painted the exact replica of the dessert plate and we adapted the other items in the five-piece place setting to go with this original reference. I found that it was much more difficult to balance all the colors to match the original painting, as numerous silk screens are used to print this pattern. It mixes well with most of the colors in the Lace pattern to set a beautiful table or buffet. The flatware is from Alain Saint-Joanis.

LEFT AND OPPOSITE The vibrantly colored plate in the Peacock pattern, placed on an embroidered silk table runner from India, was conceived by my daughter Dana, and painted by Wendy Rahn in 2010. The cobalt blue lines in the tail feathers are underlaid with a wash of green, turquoise, and other colors that are intriguing to look at. Even though the motif includes a false gold for the sparkle, the pattern is microwavable and dishwasher-safe. The bamboo flatware is from Alain Saint-Joanis.

OVERLEAF The dining area in the bay-windowed alcove of the kitchen, has been furnished with a table and chairs, made of cherry and beech in 2007 by Thos. Moser. The ship model is supposed to be a likeness of the HMS Endeavour, British Royal Navy research vessel that Lieutenant James Cook commanded to Australia and New Zealand on his first voyage of discovery from 1768 to 1771. It was made in 1924 and I bought it at an antique consignment shop in York, Maine.

OPPOSITE Our Boston Harbor bowl was designed in the 1980s, exclusively for Shreve, Crump & Low, the famous Boston luxury retail shop. The bowl is entitled the "Birthplace of American Commerce" and depicts Boston Harbor in 1800. The design is based on an interpretation of a lithograph by De Roy after a drawing by A.J. Milbert from the early 1800s. Clipper ships were built in Maine, with 90 dating from 1850 to 1856, according to William Hutchinson Rowe, the American author and historian from Yarmouth, Maine. The Nightingale clipper ship, depicted here, was one of the fastest in the world, designed and built at the Hanscom Shipyard in Eliot, Maine, in 1851 by Samuel Hanscom, Jr.

RIGHT The Blue Torquay pattern, created around 1820, was inspired by the sea and the elegant resort town of Torquay, which clings to the coast of Devon in south west England and is known for its mild climate and abundant marine life. The shells and entwined sea grasses were an inspiration for the Swansea potters who flourished in the region between 1764 and 1846.

PREVIOUS PAGES Our Carp tureen is an exact reproduction of a monumental tureen, which dates from 1740–1760, and was photographed on the rocks in front of the main house. It is one of the oldest objects in the Mottahedeh collection. Although it is meant to be a tureen, it is hard to imagine serving soup in it. Besides the dramatic sweep of its body and its lustrous coral color with touches of gold, this sculpture defies the essential nature of hard porcelain, which is to slump in the kiln when the ceramic fuses to glass. It is a testament to the ceramist's art from every perspective. In Chinese culture, the carp represents success and plenty.

OPPOSITE AND RIGHT I consider the Waterdance fish service design, which expresses fluidity, a tour de force. The fish were taken from Chinese watercolor paintings in the library at the Winterthur Museum, Garden & Library in Winterthur, Delaware. The transparent feel of the work on paper was captured in the entirely different medium of ceramics. But images on paper do not always translate well to glassy ceramics as one's eye perceives them differently. Paper absorbs light and ceramics reflect light. As I wanted to express the translucent nature of water and the feel of watercolor, we added touches of silvery mica to catch the light on the bodies of the fish. This is one of the many technical accomplishments of the Leipold ceramic screenprinting company in Germany. I was first attracted to the carp and then looked for other fish in the library that could work well on the serving pieces. We developed a fish platter, oval servers, two deep round bowls, and small oval dishes, all with new shapes. For the decoration around the edge of the pieces, I envisioned waving seagrass to go with the concept of fluidity. This pattern is microwavable and dishwasher-safe, so I use the plates and serving pieces every day when we are in Kittery.

RIGHT Our Swan pattern, in salmon, is also fluid in concept, and was set up in our garden. It is an updated version of the iconic Swan Service, the original of which was produced at Meissen, the first European porcelain factory, in Saxony. The first Swan Service of 2,200 pieces was commissioned in 1737 for Count Heinrich Brühl, the director of the Meissen factory. Former Vice-President Nelson Rockefeller purchased some of the original plates and commissioned Mottahedeh to make the dinnerware as well as a tea service.

OPPOSITE I love trees, especially if they have outlived us by a century or so, like this majestic oak that stands tall in front of our house.

RIGHT Chelsea Porcelain Works was at the birth of English porcelain manufacture in London in 1745. It was next to the four-acre Chelsea Physic Garden, established as the Apothecaries Garden in 1673 by the Worshipful Society of Apothecaries, to grow medicinal plants. A number of years ago I was asked to speak there. Before I came to the company, Mottahedeh's Chelsea Botanicals dinnerware—a pattern that is now retired—was developed with the Metropolitan Museum of Art in New York. The service was decorated with adaptations of famous botanical illustrations made by the Chelsea factory. Sir Hans Sloane, physician to King George III, had commissioned paintings of newly arrived Chinese plants in the Chelsea Physic Garden and these were later translated into dinnerware patterns. While in London, I met Susie Ray, who was an expert of botanical painting. She was commissioned to draw four different deciduous trees and their nuts: the mighty oak and the little acorn, chestnut, pecan, and hazelnut. We call the pattern Nutleaf. The set of four dessert plates has matching cups and saucers and an oak cake plate, all dappled with gold flecks around their rims.

II. HISTORIC COLLECTIONS

"We are fortunate to have so many long and respected relationships with historical societies, foundations, and museums. I'm continuously surprised to see Mottahedeh treasures being rediscovered. I went through our files and came up with 22 associations and several hundred designs. Because these associations are so extensive, we have focused here on four with the broadest collections representing the history of decorative arts in America: Mount Vernon, George Washington's home, in Mount Vernon, Virginia; Henry du Pont's American decorative arts collection at the Winterthur Museum, Garden, and Library in Winterthur, Delaware; Historic Charleston Foundation in Charleston, South Carolina; and Colonial Williamsburg, in Williamsburg, Virginia. We are primarily showing the designs that have endured or have been developed over the past 30 years. When people read this book, I have no doubt that letters and calls will come about what I left out because the number of products not represented is vast. I beg your indulgence if one of your favorites is missing!"—Wendy

MOUNT VERNON, VIRGINIA

"For a period of time our relationship with Mount Vernon was dormant until we were reacquainted through Beverly Addington, the product development director at the time. She served a lovely intimate lunch in the Garden House—the Mount Vernon arboretum—and then took me to visit the archeology office where they showed me some excavated ceramic dinnerware and glassware shards. Through their research, it was determined that the Washingtons had used English Staffordshire salt glaze stoneware for their dinners. I was fascinated. A fine friendship was born, and from it, the reintroduction of the centuries-old design we call Prosperity, only this time it appeared as a bright white, delicate, and intricate porcelain."—Wendy

"The Mansion at Mount Vernon—the home of George Washington and his wife, Martha, is one of the most iconic 18th-century residences in America. It was ten times the size of the average home in Colonial Virginia and was expanded over several years. The Mount Vernon Ladies Association has been maintaining the estate since they acquired it from the Washington family in 1858. Our collaboration with Mount Vernon was enhanced by the opportunity to make licensed products for the State Department in Washington, DC. We called it the Diplomatic Service. It was a group of objects featuring the early American eagle paired with blue-and-white Fitzhugh borders and trimmed in gold. These were designed for American embassies around the world. Over the years, we made many items under the Mount Vernon license, such as giftwares, which represented the 13 original American colonies as well as other colonial and historically accurate styles. The reinterpretation of 18th-century style holds great significance in today's world, enabling us to delve into the background of studying the objects and designs from that era. By the period's design, origin, and consumption patterns, we gain valuable insights into the lives and experiences of the Washington family, the enslaved individuals, and others who lived and toiled on the estate. The reinterpretation of 18th-century style connects the past to the present, enhancing our understanding of its social and cultural context. Through this process, we can preserve and pay homage to the rich history of our society and its enduring legacy."
—**Susan Hoffman**, director of retail and licensing, Mount Vernon

PAGE 93 Clockwise from top left: The front parlor at Mount Vernon has a tufted camelback sofa upholstered in Saxon Blue silk damask. A newly woven Wilton carpet replicates the original; the original Hong bowl from 1780-1790, is on display at the Winterthur Museum, Garden & Library. The portraits are by Rembrandt Peale, *left*, and James Frothingham, *right*; the dramatic three-story, cantilevered flying staircase in Charleston's Nathaniel Russell House dates from 1808; the 1695 Nelson-Galt House is believed to be the oldest residential dwelling in Colonial Williamsburg.

PREVIOUS PAGES RIGHT A tall, creamware jar in Mottahedeh's Greek Key pattern is a bright spot in the formal front parlor, a room full of saturated color, which is one of the finest examples of Colonial Virginia architecture. The swagged and tasseled curtains have been recreated in a Saxon Blue silk damask. A neoclassical mirror, purchased for the house in 1790, was one of Martha Washington's favorite pieces. The reflection is of Charles Wilson Peale's 1772 portrait of General George Washington.

OPPOSITE Washington's two-story high New Room is the grandest space in the house. The detailed architectural ornamentation, stylish furnishings, and vivid paint and wallpaper expressed the finest tastes of the era. Mottahedeh's Creamware latticework urns, flanked by two knife boxes, rest on a sideboard made in 1797 by John Aitken, the Philadelphia cabinetmaker. The space served many functions, from hosting large dinners to being used as a picture gallery.

RIGHT Pieces on the sideboard, in the vividly painted green dining room, include a large tureen and platter in Mottahedeh's Prosperity pattern. The delicately decorated stoneware collection was inspired by salt-glazed fragments excavated in Mount Vernon.

LEFT The magnificent blue-and-white National Trust presentation or punch bowl, displayed in the dining room, was adapted from a Chinese Export bowl at Cliveden, near Philadelphia, and a property of the National Trust for Historic Preservation. It expresses the Blue Canton style around 1790. Punch, a mixture of fruit juices and sometimes alcohol, was often served to guests from a large bowl and poured into small cups with handles.

OPPOSITE In 1785, the dining room was painted in a striking verdigris green, the color said to be "grateful to the eye" and with its additional coat of glaze, less likely to fade. The table is set as it might have been for a small dinner, using Mottahedeh's Cincinnati service, an exact reproduction of George Washington's most famous set of china, originally produced and decorated in Canton, China, in 1784 and brought to America on the first United States ship to enter the China trade. The service was purchased for Washington by General Henry Lee. Washington was the first president general of the society whose mission was to recognize the honorable services of French and American officers during the American Revolution. There are two versions of the plate's center motifs, both of which are licensed products of the Winterthur Museum. A collection of classical and military themed etchings surround the room. A graphic, painted floorcloth adds a contemporary touch to the 18th-century room.

OPPOSITE Two complementary patterns reproduced by Mottahedeh include a cookie plate, *top*, in Mandarin Bouquet, a pattern adapted from an 18th-century Chinese Export Hong Bowl with a bouquet in a basket in the center, and a leaf tray, *bottom*, in George Washington's Cincinnati service, its center representing the winged figure of Fame carrying the insignia of the Society of Cincinnati. Both are surrounded by the classic blue and white Fitzhugh border.

RIGHT Various pieces in blue-and-white patterns created by Mottahedeh are displayed in the butler's pantry. Adjacent to the dining room, it was used to store the everyday china and porcelain. Also included are pieces by Mottahedeh in other blue-and-white patterns.

LEFT The third floor of the house included bedrooms and storage rooms. In the northeast garret room, a small fireplace was added in 1776. Formerly the chambers were heated solely by heat rising from fires burned in the chimneys below.

OPPOSITE Pieces from Mottahedeh's Creamware and Prosperity collections are shown in the Bull's Eye Room (china closet) that is noted for its large oval window, the focal point of the west pediment of the house. The shelving is original to the house. An inventory from 1799 confirms that the space was used for storage as it was listed as the "China Closet Upstairs." It is believed that George Washington had a deep affinity for stoneware and creamware and used it extensively at Mount Vernon.

OVERLEAF A Prosperity tureen sits on the work table in the kitchen that was used to prepare all the meals for the Washingtons and their frequent guests. It was placed in a separate building from the main house in order to avoid excessive heat, the risks of fire, and cooking odors. In addition, the outbuilding separated the domestic functions of the enslaved cooks and servants from the activities of the family living nearby. Under Martha Washington's supervision, the cooks planned each day's menus, selected ingredients, and oversaw food preparation. Enslaved laborers on the estate grew and harvested most of the Washingtons' food which included wheat and corn from the fields, fresh vegetables from the garden, fruits form the orchards, fish caught in the Potomac River, and smoked ham from hogs raised on the site. Imported luxuries like tea, coffee, chocolate, olives, oranges, and wine supplemented the homegrown ingredients.

THE WINTERTHUR MUSEUM, GARDEN & LIBRARY, WINTERTHUR, DELAWARE

"Henry Francis du Pont's unique appreciation of beauty and history created this premier decorative arts museum. It represents truly historic and American style. It shows how one person can have a tremendous impact on our understanding of our shared culture."—Wendy

"Winterthur Museum, Garden & Library, the premier museum of American decorative arts, has an unparalleled collection of nearly 90,000 objects made or used in America since 1640. The collection is displayed in the magnificent 175-room house, much as it was when the family of founder Henry Francis du Pont called it home.

Winterthur builds upon the vision of Henry Francis du Pont to inspire and educate through its collection, estate, and academic programs by engaging diverse audiences in the study, preservation, and interpretation of American material culture, art, design, and history.

In September of 1977, the Winterthur Board of Trustees adopted a five-point program "to maintain [Winterthur's] position of leadership as an educational center in the field of American decorative arts and material culture." The Winterthur collection, the trustees decided, should be made "more widely known and more easily accessible to the interested public..., maintaining at all times a quality level of interpretation." As a means to achieve these ends, public outreach programs and cost-effective management were coupled with "an effective development program designed to broaden the base of support."

Mottahedeh was chosen as the ceramic licensee based on demonstrated excellence in design and manufacturing. The Winterthur collection of licensed products was launched in 1982 with Mottahedeh as one of 12 hallmark licenses. The reproduction of the Winterthur Hong bowl was an extraordinary project. The exceptionally large and beautiful bowl is decorated with pictures of Western hongs at Canton, including those of the United States, Sweden, Great Britain, France, and Spain. Mottahedeh is probably the only manufacturer of porcelain in the world who could have undertaken a project of such scale and refinement as this reproduction. More than two years were spent developing a prototype. An undecorated porcelain bowl was created in China that had, like the original, a smooth rounded base. Connoisseurs of Chinese porcelain always look for a smooth base or "foot" when evaluating quality. A kiln of extraordinary size was found to accommodate the exact size of the original bowl. To create an accurate decal or special plate, the director of Winterthur licensing flew with the Hong bowl to Germany, buying the priceless antique its own seat on the plane. The plate, which took nine months to engrave, was made from the original design. The decorative elements were separated into 27 colors for fidelity of reproduction. The colors were applied to the plate, one at a time, with three days of drying time between each application of color. After determining the acceptability of the coloration, patterns were made from the colored plate, applied to the bowl, and fired.

This reproduction has been called "the bowl of the century." It fully captures the spirit of the original, one of the finest and rarest designs ever created for export from China. The original bowl with its pictures of 13 Western hongs is displayed in the Phyfe Room at Winterthur. Working with Wendy Kvalheim and her staff is a delight. Wendy's training and talent for design makes a collaboration an assurance of an excellent product. Her insistence on bringing a beautifully crafted and saleable product to market is a major contributor to the 41-year length of the Mottahedeh/Winterthur partnership!"

—**Kris DeMesse**, director of product development, Winterthur Museum, Garden & Library

PREVIOUS PAGES RIGHT The Order of Cincinnati was the noteworthy dinnerware pattern in Winterthur's first collection. This pattern is a reproduction of an original from a Chinese Export porcelain dinner service made for George Washington, around 1786. The central motif is a figure representing "Fame" holding the insignia of the Society of Cincinnati, of which George Washington was the first president—a fraternal order of French and American officers who served in the American Revolution. Winterthur owns 66 pieces of this dinner service that once graced the tables of Mount Vernon, the largest number in any public or private collection.

LEFT During the late 18th and early 19th centuries, factories or hongs in China, served western traders as warehouses, offices, and residences. The trading system was established in 1757 by the Qing Dynasty to eliminate contact between the Chinese people and "foreign devils." This large and beautiful punch bowl is a Mottahedeh reproduction for Winterthur, of an original Hong bowl that dates from 1785 to 1800.

OPPOSITE The Chinese Parlor at Winterthur is noted for its original hand-painted 18th-century Chinese wallpaper panels. It features a superb collection of American furniture including a magnificent set of Chinese Chippendale chairs. The du Ponts entertained many guests in this enchanting room and also enjoyed family time there, playing card games, backgammon, and listening to Ruth Wales du Pont, Henry Francis' wife, play the Steinway miniature grand piano.

OPPOSITE AND RIGHT The Tassel dessert service in the Georgia Room rests on a mahogany and marble-topped side table with brass escutcheons that dates from 1815 to 1825 and was in the collection of Henry Francis du Pont. Mottahedeh later made a reproduction of the service and included a five-piece place setting. The pieces are edged in gold. The portrait is of Oliver Hillhouse Prince, an editor, attorney, and politician, who was from a prominent Georgia family and was elected a United States senator by the Georgia State Legislature in 1828.

PREVIOUS PAGES The Winterthur Elephant candlestick pair, previously displayed in the Lake Erie Hall in the mansion, were made in China between 1850 and 1900. It is likely that the eight-inch-high porcelain figures, depicting Asian elephants, may have been designed to hold joss sticks, a form of incense used in worship and may have been intended for the Indian or Middle Eastern markets that made up a significant proportion of the China trade. They would have also been popular with the Germans and Dutch who were particularly fond of Chinese porcelain figures.

LEFT Henry Francis du Pont would regularly buy historical structures, disassemble them, and reassemble them inside Winterthur, his 175-room mansion. Along with other reconstituted buildings, he created a town square of shops and houses indoors, in what had been a badminton court. The museum's extensive antique pewter collection is displayed in the cabinet and Mottahedeh's reproduction of Blue Torquay English transferware sits on the shop counter.

OPPOSITE Over decades, we made Blue Torquay, followed by Green Torquay and finally, Coral Torquay—moving from paper transferware to lithographic prints in order to get a more consistent color in production. For that reason, we subsequently moved our production from Burgess and Leigh in England to a factory in Portugal.

OPPOSITE AND RIGHT **Mandarin Bouquet**, a charming bouquet of flowers in a basket, adapted from an 18th-century Chinese Hong bowl, is surrounded by a classic blue-and-white Fitzhugh border. These elements combine easily to create an elegant dinner service in the Winterthur collection.

HISTORIC CHARLESTON FOUNDATION, CHARLESTON, SOUTH CAROLINA

"South Carolina, was one of the 13 original American colonies and Charleston today is a thriving, pretty, and historic town. The Historic Charleston Foundation differs from other museum foundations we have worked with as they have connected the local residents of historic homes to interact with the product development teams. These residents have offered the use of their objects as prototypes and their royalties support the foundation. We have been welcomed into their homes, marveled at the inventive and beautiful ways they made a historic structure fit in with contemporary life, and have made it their own."—Wendy

Celebrating its 75th anniversary in 2022, Historic Charleston Foundation has a long history of saving houses and buildings at risk through advocacy as well as their Revolving Fund which purchases such properties and sells them to preservation-minded buyers. Partnering with major manufacturers of distinctive furnishings, fine china, and decorative accessories, the foundation initiated their Reproductions Program. The goal was to faithfully reproduce pieces for sale to provide royalties to support ongoing preservation efforts.

Two of the most popular styles of Chinese Export china were Sacred Bird & Butterfly and Blue Canton. Both are reproduced by Mottahedeh. The origins of the original Blue Canton pattern used for reproduction came from the private collection of Dr. Fraser Wilson, a foundation board member and well-respected collector of fine furnishing and decorative accessories. Historic Charleston Foundation has partnered with Mottahedeh on numerous product introductions over the past 50 years including fine china, casual porcelain patterns, as well as brass.

When Historic Charleston Foundation became interested in a reproductions program in 1971, Alison Harwood, who was senior editor of *Vogue* and board member of the foundation, contacted Mildred Mottahedeh about becoming the licensee for porcelain. She and her husband Rafi came to Charleston and through Historic Charleston Foundation met Dr. Fraser Wilson, a physician who had been collecting blue-and-white Chinese Export porcelain since he was 12 years old. He and his family lived in a large 1820s Charleston single house and he had every shape of Blue Canton imaginable. It was very entertaining to be present as Fraser opened cabinet after crammed cabinet, showing his treasures. Mildred and Fraser had a lifelong friendship thereafter.

Americans merchant ships began a direct line of trade to China shortly after the Revolutionary War and, by the end of the 18th century, had made the United States second only to England as importers of Asian goods. This was an impressive feat considering that in those days, just getting to China was a highly speculative and dangerous enterprise. Trade vessels leaving American ports took two years on average to return, if they returned at all. Ultimately, of course, the risks taken to acquire luxuries from the furthest reaches of the world only fueled the desire for them. Demand for such exotic wares as lacquered furniture, tea, silk, and, of course, porcelain, reached a fevered pitch, and Charleston merchant Nathaniel Russell was more than happy to oblige his clientele.

One of Russell's merchant ships, appropriately named *Russell* and owned in partnership with the Newport, Rhode Island, firm of Gibbs and Channing, was the only documented 18th-century vessel to have engaged in the China trade directly from Charleston. Setting sail in the spring of 1796, *Russell*'s Captain, William Wood, eventually steered the ship into the port of Canton some seven months later. There, he sought the services of Canton's leading porcelain merchant, Syngchong, from whom he purchased over 10,000 pieces. Wood and the *Russell* returned to Charleston a little over a year later, this time with a hold packed full of porcelain of varying shapes, sizes, colors, and patterns. Nathaniel Russell secured an announcement in the *South Carolina Gazette* stating that his vessel had made port in Charleston carrying a payload "direct from Canton China" that included 37,000 pounds of ceramics for the Carolina market. The licensing program allows for both faithful reproductions as well as adaptations.

A taste for hand-craftsmanship re-emerged during the last years of the 19th century and into the early 20th. Though initially seen as a movement against the Industrial Revolution and its cheap low-quality mass-production products, most American consumers preferred more artisanal, handicrafted pieces. Today, modern manufacturing techniques producing elegant, high-quality reproductions have made the look and feel of historical pieces more widely available and at the same time convey the importance of preservation in terms of material culture.

—**Grahame Long**, director of museums, and **Cornelia Pelzer**, former director of product development

PREVIOUS PAGES RIGHT A tea service in Blue Canton, decorated with views of China, has been set up in the withdrawing room on the second floor of the 19th-century Nathaniel Russell House. The pattern has been a favorite for centuries. Pagodas, bridges, and landscapes appear in finely shaded cobalt blues, recreating the design of the original export wares. The most fashionable tables in the early American republic were set with blue-and-white "Canton" or "Nanking" wares, which were named for the great Chinese trading ports from which they came. Tea services made of porcelain were well known in the 18th century.

RIGHT The Withdrawing Room in the Federal-style Nathaniel Russell House features neoclassical architectural details, the highlight of which is the 22-karat gold leaf cornice that surrounds the 14½-foot-high ceiling. All of the furnishings and decorations in the house date from 1808 to 1820, when the wealthy merchant, Nathaniel Russell, lived there. Pieces of note include the neo-Classical settee, one of only six known to be made in Charleston, and the Hepplewhite-style and the mahogany Pembroke table, which was also made in Charleston.

OPPOSITE Painted in vibrant, historic, Verditer Blue, the dining room on the first floor, is one of three oval rooms in the house. The Hepplewhite-style mahogany dining table, with its center drop-leaf section and two detachable half-round ends, is surrounded by neo-Classical mahogany dining chairs, all made in Charleston around 1800 to 1810. The swags, edged in Egyptian silk tassels, are reproductions made by the textile historian, Natalie Larson, in a style that was popular in the 19th century.

RIGHT The Sacred Bird & Butterfly pattern in orange was reproduced from original designs in the Historic Charleston Foundation collection and has been popular for years. The new blue colorway never existed in colonial days and, with an agreement with Historic Charleston, is newly introduced by Mottahedeh. In the dining room of the the Nathaniel Russell House, we set the table with Sacred Bird Blue. We felt that the new colorway would be a welcome addition, so we strove for the same translucent effect of the original Sacred Bird pattern, but with silver instead of gold lines. The Chinese word for butterfly, *dié*, is a pun which expresses the wish that the owner might live to a ripe old age.

LEFT This historic, 1820 house on Lamboll Street, was restored and decorated by Alexandre Fleuren of Design AFI, based in Charleston. The walls in the Gentleman's Suite are covered in indigo blue grasscloth. Framed metal sleeve patterns from around 1890 hang above the mantel. Mottahedeh's Bamboo garniture, on the mantel, in cobalt blue, is a long-time licensed product of the Historic Charleston Foundation. A garniture is a number of matching but not identical objects intended to be displayed together.

OPPOSITE In Charleston, people are living gracefully in historic houses and they make them their own through the melding of contemporary design with the historic. The hand-painted mural in the entry foyer reflects the plant life in the gardens and winds upward along the grand staircase through the three floors. Arched doorways lead to the back of the house and to the formal dining room, which has steel and glass walls, giving the space the feeling of a conservatory. A Mottahedeh blue-and-white Canton ginger jar rests on a Venetian console in front of a Murano glass mirror.

OVERLEAF A garniture of Mottahedeh blue-and-white bamboo open and covered vases adorn the marble mantle in one of the bedrooms, which is original to the 200-year-old house.

LEFT The glass-enclosed dining room is furnished with a contemporary, grey slab table and traditional silver-painted cane chairs upholstered in orange fabric. The table is set with a mixture of china patterns that include Mottahedeh's Waterdance, which features touches of silver and gold—a nod to the colorful gardens that surround the house, and the abundant supply of local seafood served in many Charleston dishes. The flowers are arranged in a long, low bank of blooms that run the full length of the table center.

OPPOSITE This lovely Bird Creamware tureen and stand was reproduced in Italy from an 18th-century French original that was made by the renowned Pont aux Choux factory in Paris. The remarkable reproduction was made from molds taken from the antique collection at the Musée des Arts Décoratifs in Paris.

OPPOSITE The original dining room of the house has now become the primary bedroom suite. The handpainted, cane-backed bed is dressed in linens from Italy, Belgium, and America. Complementing the warm color palette are pieces from Sacred Bird & Butterfly, Mottahedeh's long-standing pattern with the Historic Charleston Foundation, which include a four-lobed cachepot, a dessert bowl, and shell dish. The Chinese Export pattern from about 1800 features an all-over design of motifs rendered with characteristic understatement and translucency in the traditional Chinese orange and gold colors. The marriage of shape and design was a success and was reproduced in English china thereafter.

RIGHT In the powder room, the house's original arched, frosted glass windows are reflected in the carved mirror. The silvery leaves on the grasscloth wallcovering echo the delicate window tracery and continue the garden theme. I love every aspect of this powder room—the coral tones of the marble, the delicacy of the fixtures, the touches of coral and silver in the mirror, the leaded half-round window, and, of course, our Sacred Bird & Butterfly tea flask, Shang vase, and porcelain soap dish.

COLONIAL WILLIAMSBURG, WILLIAMSBURG, VIRGINIA

"One aspect of our relationship with Williamsburg that I have enjoyed is working closely with the product development team and curators, gleaning something of their passion and extensive knowledge."—Wendy

"In the 1770s, in Williamsburg, patriot members of Virginia's House of Burgesses, including Thomas Jefferson and George Washington, moved toward revolution against Great Britain. Centuries later, the Colonial Williamsburg Foundation brings to life this story of the founding of the United States. Through careful research, preservation, and educational programming, we pursue our mission "That the future may learn from the past." Colonial Williamsburg maintains the world's largest living-history museum. Visitors engage in immersive and authentic 18th-century experiences, including exploring the Revolutionary era's contradiction between American liberty and American slavery.

The restoration of Williamsburg began with the Rev. Dr. W.A.R. Goodwin, rector of Bruton Parish Church. He shared his vision that Williamsburg could tell the story of the American Revolution with philanthropist John D. Rockefeller, Jr. and his wife, Abby Aldrich Rockefeller. A modest initiative begun in 1926 to preserve Williamsburg's 18th-century buildings blossomed into a full-scale restoration of the former colonial capital. The historic campus includes 89 original buildings, more than 500 meticulous reconstructions of lost structures, and two world-class art museums.

WILLIAMSBURG, the licensed brand of Colonial Williamsburg, has been making design history since 1936. A heritage brand with roots as deep as our country, we blend historic inspiration with modern influences to create classic and timeless home decor. The rich design archives of the Colonial Williamsburg Foundation and traditions of 18th-century artistry inspire thoughtfully curated collections of WILLIAMSBURG products.

Colonial Williamsburg and Mottahedeh signed a license in 1989 to reproduce fine dinnerware inspired by historic pieces in the Colonial Williamsburg collection. The first reproduction was an octagonal platter, originally part of a porcelain dinner service richly enameled with fruit and butterflies. Prince William Henry, Duke of Gloucester (1743-1805), brother of King George III, commissioned the service in 1770 from the Worcester Porcelain Manufactory in England. Mottahedeh soon expanded the Duke of Gloucester assortment to include a handsome dinner service and decorative accessories. The luxuriously decorated pattern has been one of Mottahedeh's most popular products.

Virginia Blue has a special link to 18th-century Williamsburg because of the history of the china that inspired it. The pattern is interpreted from a set of Chinese Export porcelain that Robert Beverley, a Virginia planter, ordered for his bride in 1762. In an era before wedding registries, he was dependent upon the taste of his London agent. Beverley's surviving letterbook [Robert Beverley Letterbook, 1761-1775, Library of Congress] reveals that he instructed his agent to send "a compleat set of China… sufficient for two genteel Courses of Victuals. . . & all the necessary Appendages for an [sic] handsome Tea Table," asking that he "chuse the China of the most fashionable Sort." Much of the service descended in the Beverley family at their estate, Blandfield, in Essex County, Virginia. Many pieces are now preserved in the Colonial Williamsburg collection.

Developing the pattern for today's tables, Wendy and I thought it should be simplified. We deconstructed the original design to feature different elements from the antique on various pieces of the service. It still needed something. Wendy's inspired idea to add a pearlized ecru surface gives a fresh patina to the antique design to make Virginia Blue sing on today's tables.

Mildred Mottahedeh donated to Colonial Williamsburg a Chinese Export porcelain soup plate to serve as inspiration for our Imperial Blue pattern. The antique plate was part of a large service custom-ordered from China in the 1730s through the British East India Company. The original plate bears an English coat of arms that has been omitted in the reproduction service.

The 18th century, the period to which Colonial Williamsburg is restored, was a golden age of porcelain production in England and Europe. Inspired by imported Chinese porcelains, factories competed to develop the complex technology to make exquisite china dishes. How lucky we are that Mottahedeh enables us to channel the enthusiasm of hosts of the 1700s who entertained with pride on exquisite and fashionable china.

As an incurable chinaholic, I was thrilled to be assigned as liaison for the WILLIAMSBURG license with Mottahedeh. When the license started, I was lucky to meet the legendary, fascinating, and formidable Mildred Mottahedeh and to hear from her about the origins of her business.

Beyond my pride in our products, one of the great pleasures of working with Mottahedeh has been getting to know Wendy Kvalheim. Wendy is a kindred spirit: we share cultural curiosity and a passion for travel. Over the years she and I have worked together to develop WILLIAMSBURG Mottahedeh products. I admire Wendy's business acumen and aesthetic judgment and am honored to count her as a colleague and friend."

—**Liza Gusler**, deputy director, WILLIAMSBURG Brand and Licensing, The Colonial Williamsburg Foundation

PREVIOUS PAGES RIGHT The Nelson-Galt House, built in 1695, is believed to be the oldest residential dwelling in Colonial Williamsburg. Its original owner was the governor of Virginia and a signer of the Declaration of Independence. The Galt family owned the house for the longest period of time. In the dining room, a Brighton Pavilion bird figurine takes center stage. Its design was inspired by the wallpaper in the Lightfoot House in Williamsburg. The handpainted wallpaper, "Regency Views" by Paul Montgomery, was inspired by the landscape designs of the late 18th-century Englishman, Humphrey Repton. The Brighton Pavilion bird pieces are made in an Italian factory near Venice, Italy. Although we loved the form, but not the colors, we went back and forth with the product development team at Colonial Williamsburg until we finally settled on a look that everyone was happy with. It has been a Mottahedeh favorite for more than 20 years.

RIGHT Our Chelsea Bird porcelain collection was inspired by exotic bird designs found on a set of plates in the Colonial Williamsburg collection. They are exact reproductions, as are the oval platter and the oval serving dish.

134

OPPOSITE AND RIGHT I believe that the more colors there are in a design, the higher is the possibility to have a variety of other colors work well with it. Service plates are useful for adding a color dimension to the table. This plate goes under the dinner or appetizer plate and, when the course is changed, they become pretty place holders. Here, we show two completely different treatments. Service plates are larger than dinner plates and are sometimes used for the main course.

OVERLEAF AND PAGES 140–141 When Williamsburg and Mottahedeh began working together in 1989, the first reproduction was of a small Royal Worcester platter in Williamsburg's collection, made in 1770 for the Duke of Gloucester, the brother of King George III. Thereafter, we made an exact reproduction of the full and singular antique service of this design. We used historical Worcester shapes for the serving pieces and Dan Melman, a shape designer, sculpted a tureen and stand using archival references for this effusive Rococo design with its profusion of flora, fruits, and butterflies. These items were hand-cast in Europe.

LEFT Heather Chadduck, a Birmingham, Alabama–based interior designer, was the Colonial Williamsburg Designer in Residence from 2022 to 2023, designed the table setting using Mottahedeh's Imperial Blue pattern. Imperial Blue was developed from a rimmed soup plate in the Mottahedeh collection in collaboration with Williamsburg. It was part of a large custom-made service with a coat of arms in the center, which dates from about 1730. It was ordered and delivered from China for a noble family. We developed several pieces for this service, inspired by this plate. Imperial Blue has been one of our bridal favorites and, in its simplified version, has been expanded to many more colors and shapes. The Levingston goblets are from Park Designs; the pewter goblets from Match; and the flatware is from the designer's personal collection. "The most important lesson I learned," said Chadduck, "was that there is no need to reinvent the wheel. The color palettes are here, the architectural details are here, and if you do your homework and look around, you'll realize how many decorating lessons are rooted in Colonial Williamsburg."

OPPOSITE In an upstairs bedroom, decorated by Chadduck, a small collection of Imperial Blue items sit on a side table—mugs, a small bowl, large and small covered boxes, and a keepsake tray. While mugs of this type were not used in Colonial days, Mottahedeh produced them to respond to the uses of the times we live in today. The floral design, fired in cobalt blue, is echoed in the wallpaper.

LEFT AND OPPOSITE In the study, the daybed has been covered with Schumacher's Dandridge Damask, a pattern inspired by a silk gown worn by Martha Dandridge Custis Washington. Mottahedeh's Virginia Blue china rests on a late 19th-century scalloped tea table. Virginia Blue is a great example of using an original design as inspiration for a new and different creation. The dinner plate was part of Williamsburg's extensive collection, which was originally owned by the Beverley family. We thought this plate was interesting and lively, with its scalloped edge and all linework painted in cobalt blue. The central bird and foliage motif was enlarged and lifted off the dinner plate onto the dessert plate. The dinner plate now has the original lacy border, and a plain center. The cobalt blue color was then tipped toward a periwinkle hue and the plain background of the dessert and dinner, bread, and butter plates, and cup and saucer, became a pearlized ecru, giving the china a light-catching sheen. Virginia Blue is a lacy and delicate design that we hope will have the longevity that its predecessor has enjoyed.

OPPOSITE AND RIGHT Our Creamware is a soft paste porcelain that is fired at a lower temperature than hard porcelain. Because of the low temperatures, it will hold up well in the kiln and will allow complex shapes in its design. The Bird tureen, with its hand-applied bird and flowers, is one of our longest-standing items. The pierced basket and plate are derived from a silver service. Creamware items are wonderful as decorative objects but as they cannot withstand high temperatures; it is not advisable to cook with them. The dolphin-base console belongs to Chadduck. Today, this pattern is produced primarily in Italy. We have offered many styles over the years. Most of the designs initially came from France and from the Musée des Arts Décoratifs in Paris. There was a factory near the Pont aux Choux that specialized in this type of wares, so that became the name of the style. It is very ornate with embossing, floral reliefs, and reticulated surfaces.

LEFT The wing chairs in the Queen bedroom have been upholstered with Schumacher's Jakarta linen print in greige. Schumacher, a Williamsburg licensee, was the textile sponsor for the Williamsburg Designer in Residence project. The Mottahedeh bowl is an 18th-century Fitzhugh design in iron red.

OPPOSITE A creamware pair of figurines—a Chinoiserie man playing a guitar and a lady holding a bird—catch the light on an upstairs windowsill.

III. NOT YOUR GRANDMA'S CHINA

"So many young people, especially women, have told me that they received their mother's or grandmother's china but don't use it, as they don't particularly have an affinity for it. So it remains in boxes forever. If they are young and would like to bring it out, they stop short of actually serving food on it because they feel their contemporaries wouldn't feel comfortable using it. It might also not be in fashion. But I believe that while fashions may change, style endures. Some people are greatly influenced by the prevailing taste of the day and by what others consider appropriate. Truly stylish people know, understand, and respect the rules, yet bend them to interpret as they please. The interesting feature of style is that it can put a unique spin on an old subject. My art teacher told me that one's way of making mistakes reflects the evolution of one's signature style. We propose that you take out that china, mix it up, add color, and find some unusual presentation with fabrics, flatware, and flowers. Make it your own and you will surprise and delight your guests. A beautiful and well-balanced design gives the viewer an aha! moment. You don't know why that is, but you just like it. It is a physical response. It rings like a bell. By the way, very high-quality porcelain has a sonorous ring when you tap it. Play with the elements of design—color, line, shape, form, texture, light versus dark, balance, proportion, and composition. The final design will surely be uplifting and is well worth the effort."—Wendy

PREVIOUS PAGES RIGHT Clockwise from the left: A Rookwood Sung Vase in verdigris and blue sits by an Art Deco poster in East Hampton, New York; In Palm Beach, Florida, Prosperity dinnerware is paired with a scalloped-edge napkin from Everyday Elegance; a Palma tea set and dessert plates are set out on a shelf in an apartment in Palm Beach; Barriera Corallina dinnerware by Tony Duquette and a pair of parakeets decorate the table on a Palm Beach terrace.

RIGHT AND OVERLEAF RIGHT On the terrace overlooking the swimming pool and Gardiner's Bay, a table and chairs—from David Sutherland—offer an ideal place for an al fresco meal. The table has been set with Blue Dragon plates, a symbol of the Chinese Emperor Kangxi (1622–1722). An organic-shaped tagine has also been placed on the table, and it can be used to serve the traditional Moroccan dish, gazpacho, pasta, or even a salad. Sunflowers provide a summer touch while the Blue Dragon pattern coordinates with the teak-handled flatware and rush placemats. The acrylic glasses are from Mario Luca Giusti, in Italy.

A SYMPHONY IN BLUE-AND-WHITE

"When I was growing up in Ohio, our house was all done in shades of blue as my mother loved collecting blue Delft china and cobalt blue glass and so that became my introduction to blue-and-white, a passion that I carried with me when I created my own homes, including this one that I now share with my husband, Peter Wilson, a retired corporate lawyer, in East Hampton, New York," explained the New York and Palm Beach, Florida-based interior designer Scott Sanders. *"I started collecting blue-and-white Mottahedeh pieces years ago for my first apartment in New York, as decorative objects,"* he added. *"But as time went on, I started buying more functional pieces and found not only that do the different patterns go well together but they can also be used with many other textures and materials. When you mix patterns throughout the house, something very special happens and it all works and feels quite wonderful."*—Scott Sanders

LEFT At one end of the spacious kitchen, Sanders created a modern interpretation of a traditional china cabinet where different Blue Canton porcelains are arranged in a high-gloss lacquered breakfront. Woven baskets and mid-20th-century wood pieces are also displayed. Vintage amber goblets are paired with Blue Canton china on the hand-crafted table by David Iatesta from John Rosselli & Associates in New York.

OPPOSITE Sanders likes to combine the Blue Canton and Blue Shòu china and the vintage amber glasses he collected years ago with other decorative pieces, letting the different patterns and shapes play off each other.

OVERLEAF Blue Canton was not so much a pattern as a genre, and the Chinese artisans painted many designs over the years. All cobalt blue-and-white pieces can be mixed together. The combinations are endless.

OPPOSITE A set of vintage ceramic canisters act as a backdrop for two Blue Canton serving pieces that are as useful as they are pretty as they can go into the dishwasher as well as the microwave.

RIGHT AND OVERLEAF A vintage table by Warren Platner for Knoll and chairs from Ralph Pucci anchor the dining area in a corner of the living room. The table is set with Emmeline, an in-glaze, high-fired dinner pattern in cobalt blue. The deep blue flowers are set off with the bright white plate for a fresh look. The underplate is Lexington, a hand-painted service plate in azure by Robert Haviland & C. Parlon, Limoges. Other accessories include More Fire Glass bottles by Elizabeth Lyons. The painting is by Andrew Masullo.

LEFT Tea is served—using Mottahedeh's Blue Dragon china—in a corner of the living room under a photograph by Irish artist Richard Mosse. A curved sofa, custom-designed by Scott Sanders LLC, surrounds a vintage table by Eero Saarinen and a vintage chair by the American designer Edward Wormley. The lamp is from the Urban Electric Company. The custom-made wool rug designed by Scott Sanders LLC has a pattern of repeating stripes that are reminiscent of waves in the ocean.

OPPOSITE The Blue Dragon tea service is a great mix of modern and traditional elements. The dragon illustration and the scale of the design on the saucers are reproductions of dishes that date back to the 17th century. The original dragon design has been applied to the modern shapes of the teapot, creamer, and sugar bowl.

JUXTAPOSING CLASSICISM WITH MODERNISM

"Twenty years ago, I moved into my apartment at the Apthorp, on the Upper West Side of Manhattan, embarked on a gut renovation, and took everything down to the studs," recalled Jennifer Post, a former New York–based interior designer, who now lives part of the year in Palm Beach, Florida. *"I then installed a series of 10-foot-high slabs of Blanco Dolomite, a Turkish marble. My dream was to have the most elegant white-on-white surfaces using different materials— from the stone, with its white with grey veining, the custom-made white-painted millwork, and the Venetian plaster walls."* The hues, she added, *"are all soft whites that bounce harmoniously off each other—some are textured, some are shiny, some are flat. I call it the dancing white apartment."* Having always loved sculpture, paintings, and animals, *"I added artworks that would give the spaces humanity and color, making the art the hero of the apartment."* Setting a formal table, *"I especially like the juxtaposition of the antique-looking china with the modernist look of the space, and, of course, the animals that decorate the china, and the stylish stags that add just the right note to the whole setting."*—Jennifer Post

PAGES 166–167 The Apthorp's leafy courtyard offers Jennifer Post a moment of serenity in the midst of the commotion of New York City.

PREVIOUS PAGES RIGHT In a corner of Jennifer Post's all-white living room, a 19½-inch-high Mottahedeh Rookwood Classic vase in red with a traditional black vellum glaze has been placed near an etching by the American artist Robert Motherwell. The vintage French chair has been reupholstered in an Italian linen.

OPPOSITE The clean, white interior creates a powerful backdrop for antique-looking porcelain and ceramics. One of British sculptor Lynn Chadwick's seated bronzes anchors a shelf in the living room next to Mottahedeh's Wufu cachepot with its brilliant bursts of colorful lilies and a Wufu bowl. The painting is by the American artist Russell Sharon.

RIGHT The low round Wufu bowl is an exact reproduction of a Chinese Qing dynasty bowl. The peaches represent immortality and the bats represent the Five Blessings—health, wealth, virtue, a long life, and a peaceful end.

PREVIOUS PAGES, OPPOSITE, AND RIGHT
In Post's all-white dining room, the large canvas, in hues of black and gold, is by the Scottish artist Callum Innis. The black Windsor-style chair is the one Post's mother received as a Fulbright scholar. The black-and-gold-themed table, with its black glass top, is the perfect foil for the elegant porcelains, in shades of black, grey, and gold, which are reproductions of the famed Jagd porcelain service made by DuPaquier Porcelain in Vienna, Austria, around 1730. The only other competing factory in Europe was Meissen in Saxony. It discovered the recipe for making porcelain, guarded by the Chinese for centuries. DuPaquier reproductions include a set of four luncheon plates, *right*, and a platter, *opposite*, all decorated with grisaille forest animals and 22-karat gold. Here, they are paired with two sizes of our Italian-made black matte glazed Noble stag tureens with hand-painted gold accents and brass antlers. "I love how the stags look poised and sophisticated, and fit in so well in my apartment," said Post.

OVERLEAF The originals of the curly tailed pair of hand-painted bulldogs, with their custom leather collars adorned with 22-karat gold bells that date back to the mid-1700s, were found at Chatsworth, the home of the Duke of Devonshire in Derbyshire Dales, England, and now part of the Stately Homes of England Collection. The portrait of Post's beloved Boston terrier Annabelle was painted by Jim Maynard, her godfather and a captain in the United States Navy.

WHEN OPULENCE MEETS MINIMALISM

"In my light-filled apartment in Palm Beach, Florida—designed by New York–based architect David Mann—that has a panoramic view of the Atlantic Ocean, I have tried to have a minimum of furniture and added decorations to keep the environment as open and airy as possible," said Barbara Toll, a New York and Palm Beach-based art advisor and former gallerist. "The result is a very serene and very quiet space. But the introduction of the ornate Mottahedeh pieces, with their gilding and notes of fantasy have really livened up the whole space, from the all-white wraparound balcony, to the stark dining area, where a wonderful link was created between the spareness of the space and the artworks that hang on the walls."—Barbara Toll

PAGES 178–179 AND PREVIOUS PAGES
RIGHT A Tea for Two set in the Lace pattern sits on a Janus et Cie table on the terrace that encircles Barbara Toll's apartment. Glittery Hydrangea placemats by Kim Seybert frame the Butterfly Lace dessert plates; the dip-dyed napkins are also by Kim Seybert.

LEFT In the dining area, Palma, one of Mottahedeh's most opulent patterns, was an unusual choice for the white, minimalist space, yet seems to be an inspiring selection. Fyodor Solntsev, who designed most of the Kremlin and many cathedrals across eastern Europe, created the Kremlin Service for Tsar Nicholas I based on the cloisonné enamel and gold plates and dishes from the collections of the Kremlin Armory, which had been made for Tsar Alexis from 1645–1676, the father of Peter the Great. Real gold is used for all the scroll work, and the center is reminiscent of a Celtic design from the British Isles. The Radiate placemats and chain-link napkin ring are by Kim Seybert; the napkin is from Sferra; and the blue goblet is from Kartell.

OPPOSITE In the airy, open plan living room, a table from B&B Italia has been set up for a buffet. The sculpture is by the Berlin-based American artist David Adamo.

OVERLEAF For a formal dinner, the plates have been set on scalloped-linen placemats with matching napkins, all by Alex Papachristidis for the Everyday Elegance Collection. All the glassware is from Zafferano America. The Cab chairs are by the Italian architect Mario Bellini for Cassina. The paintings are by American artist Louise Fishman, on the left, and Danish-born artist Sergei Jensen, on the right.

OPPOSITE The pair of Mottahedeh Chatsworth terriers are in the Stately Homes of England Collection. The originals were crafted by Johann Joachim Kaendler, who joined the Meissen factory in 1731 and was its chief modeler from 1733 until his death in 1775. He is widely considered to be the greatest porcelain sculptor of all time and is particularly famous for his wonderfully spirited bird and animal figures. These Bolognese terriers, a breed much fancied as pets in the aristocratic households of 18th-century Europe, were reproduced from original antiques in the collection at Chatsworth House with the Stately Homes of England. Mottahedeh's reproductions are entirely hand-painted on fine porcelain in Italy.

RIGHT Sport, a Norwich terrier, has his eye on Mottahedeh's set of four Alhambra canape plates with intricate designs that were inspired by a small antique plate of Moorish style of the Alhambra, a palace in Granada, Spain. The calligraphic linework interplays with the faux wood and stone of the backgrounds. Perfect for tapas, it is available in curly pine, walnut burl, Oriental blue, and sandstone.

INTENSE COLORS IN AN ART-FILLED SPACE

"I usually try to let the art play the central role in the design of where I live," continued Barbara Toll. *"Most of the art I respond to is minimalist, yet has texture and color. My own table settings have been for the most part mainly monochrome and simply functional. When I introduced the Mottahedeh place settings to my spare loft in New York's Soho neighborhood, where I have lived for decades and which was renovated a few years ago by David Mann, it took me a little time to get used to them. But their beauty and richness really set off the simplicity of my dining room table. Its red surface has been intensified by the deep hues of the china and given me a whole new perspective on the overall feeling of the loft space."*—Barbara Toll

PAGES 188–189 The large square dining table, that Barbara Toll bought at an antiques shop in Soho in the 1980s, has been set with Starburst Medallion in the malachite and lapiz hues that complement the colors of the work by the American painter Mary Heilmann hanging on the wall. The flatware is by Achille Castiglioni for Alessi, and the glasses are from Moretti. The vintage chairs are by the Paris-based designers Elisabeth Garouste and Mattia Bonetti and the small sculpture that serves as a centerpiece is by the American artist Kiki Smith.

PREVIOUS PAGES RIGHT Mottahedeh's Starburst Medallion dinnerware, with its deep jewel tones and geometric motifs, by the legendary American designer Tony Duquette, seemed to fit in well with both the downtown loft space and the art that Toll collects. Hutton Wilkinson, the Los Angeles–based CEO and creative director of Tony Duquette, Inc. explained that Duquette, "was an iconic American designer, who as a young man, made costumes and sets for Fred Astaire musicals at MGM." Wilkinson added that Duquette, when he was in his eighties, created jewelry for Tom Ford at Gucci, and was known to have a fetish for malachite and lapis lazuli. "The idea," he said, "was to create a set of china that looked like inlaid pietra dura." The central motif of a gold outlined sunburst or starburst also reflects one of Duquette's favorite motifs. "We particularly like to mix the malachite and lapiz colors together," said Wilkinson. Toll agreed.

LEFT AND OPPOSITE The deep red lacquered surface of the dining table serves as a perfect background for the Starburst Medallion in the Red Tortoise colorway. With its inlaid details of ivory-like and black onyx-like details, it was one of Duquette's favorites. A detail of a fabric piece by the American artist Anna Betbeze can be see on the adjoining wall.

FABULOUS FLORALS IN A CHARTREUSE ROOM

"Mario Buatta, my mentor and friend, always spoke about bringing the garden indoors and that is exactly what the Tobacco Leaf pattern does," said Emily Evans Eerdmans, a design historian who worked with the late famous and fabulous interior designer on Mario Buatta: 50 Years of American Interior Decoration, *and who, as the founder of Eerdmans New York, a fine art and decorative arts gallery, hosts salons, book signings, art exhibitions, and garden parties in her landmarked New York Greenwich Village Greek Revival townhouse. "While the moldings in the dining room are all original, the chartreuse lacquered walls are very much not! It was one of Mario's favorite colors. Mario was also an enormous lover and collector of Mottahedeh china. He shared the company's belief that if you couldn't own the 18th-century original, then a superior reproduction was just as satisfactory."*—Emily Evans Eerdmans

PAGES 194–195 In Emily Evans Eerdmans' chartreuse-painted dining room, the table is set with Tobacco Leaf, a prized Chinese Export pattern that was first developed around 1780, probably for the Portuguese and Brazilian markets, although some examples have been found in Europe and North America. The design includes the leaves of the flowering *Nicotiana*, or tobacco plant, upon which a small phoenix perches with a flowering twig in its beak. A pair of 19th-century Swedish beaded crystal sconces hang above two framed drawings by the British muralist Lucinda Oakes.

PREVIOUS PAGES RIGHT A Lexington service plate in Celadon from the French company, Robert Haviland & C. Parlon, holds two Tobacco Leaf plates, the whole complemented by the printed silk tablecloth made from a flower-bedecked textile from Lorca Fabrics, an English firm.

OPPOSITE An oversized Divina vase, and flowers and glassware in shades of pink and blue, complement the multicolor Tobacco Leaf dessert and dinner plates. The tureens, including a snail-topped, lettuce-covered piece, are vintage Mottahedeh pieces that were in Mario Buatta's collection but are no longer in production. The antique ivory and bone pagodas are part of Eerdmans' collection.

RIGHT A Regency convex mirror hangs above the mantelpiece in the dining room. Pieces in the Tobacco Leaf pattern include a pomegranate box and stand, a ginger jar, the Divina vase, and a rabbit tureen hand-painted in Italy. A vintage Mottahedeh cachepot with a floral motif, made in Italy, has been filled with bright pink ranunculus.

GARDEN AND WATER HUES IN A DELIGHTFUL SETTING

"Our house is modern, and I'm used to having everything that is clean and simple, but I really love blue things and feel that they look wonderful in a contemporary setting, especially out on the deck," said Mario Nievera, a landscape designer who is based in Palm Beach, Florida, and New York. Nievera's terrace, in a townhouse at The Reef that he shares with his husband, Travis Howe, a media executive, is special—perched on the Intercoastal Waterway and a delightful spot on which to enjoy a casual lunch, a break for tea, or a formal dinner. "The seaside location complements the blue of the water, and because I'm always attracted to things in nature, the green table setting becomes very much part of this lush tropical landscape. And, for everyday, I especially like elegant, all-white dishes that go so well with our contemporary furniture."—Mario Nievera

PAGES 200–201 AND PREVIOUS PAGES RIGHT On the terrace that overlooks the Intracoastal Waterway, against a rich green backdrop of plants, Mario Nievera has prepared the table for an impromptu brunch, and set up a tray for an intimate tea at sunset with Malachite, one of the patterns designed for Mottahedeh by Tony Duquette. Duquette's trademark compass star is boldly featured in lapis lazuli that contrasts with the bright green malachite-patterned plates. All the table linens are by Alex Papachristidis for the Everyday Elegance Collection.

OPPOSITE AND RIGHT For a more casual waterside meal, the table has been set with Blue Canton, a versatile pattern with over 100 items. Here it is paired with Caspari placemats in a Chinoiserie motif and blue hand-blown glasses and napkins from Zafferano America.

OVERLEAF In the dining area of the all-white living room, placemats in a rich chocolate brown with white edging by Alex Papachristidis for his Everyday Elegance Collection hold pieces of Prosperity china. The pattern is based on a historical English Staffordshire form, but the same porcelain material has been made to be more functional for today as it is now dishwasher and microwave-safe. "The elegance of the craftsmanship of this pattern with its scalloped borders resonates with our contemporary interior and its round-edged furniture," said Nievera.

CELEBRATING PATTERN-ON-PATTERN IN NEW YORK

"Mixing materials, periods, and styles has always been at the heart of any interior that my husband, Michael Steinberg, a New York-based art dealer, and I have lived in for the past 45 years," said Suzanne Slesin, who—full disclosure—is the publisher and editorial director of Pointed Leaf Press, which published this book. "And, I guess the word 'eclectic' truly defines the look of the small apartment in the Nolita neighborhood of New York where we moved 18 months ago." At first, Tobacco Leaf, Mottahedeh's most iconic pattern, whose exuberance has been undiminished by time and, with its multicolor design of leaves and gold detailing, "seemed to have a somewhat more traditional look than one to which we would gravitate, the pattern's beautiful color palette and fine craftsmanship totally seduced us, and the china now fits in perfectly in our quite varied and pattern-on-pattern environment."—Suzanne Slesin

211

PAGES 208–209 In the dining area of the apartment, under a painting by the American artist Melissa Brown, a vintage table in the style of the 1950s Italian designer Ico Parisi has been set with Mottahedeh Tobacco Leaf and Lace plates, all within a complementary palette. The Hybrid glassware is from Seletti, an Italian company; the vase is a vintage piece by the Italian architect Sergio Asti for Knoll; and the plant stand is by the French architect Pierre Chareau.

PREVIOUS PAGES RIGHT A Tobacco Leaf dinner plate has been set on a Lace charger in cobalt blue; the bamboo flatware is from Alain Saint-Joanis; the goblets are from Seletti; and the 19th-century kilim rug is happily in a similar palette.

RIGHT The textured surface of the planks of a cupboard in scrapwood by the Dutch designer Piet Hein Eek functions as a background for two accessories in the Tobacco Leaf pattern: A useful cachepot and a charming leaf platter.

ARTS AND CRAFTS POTTERY IN A RUSTIC HOME

"For as long as I can remember, modern design objects—especially primary-colored china and accessories—dominated the tables my husband and I set in the series of country houses in which we spent weekends and summer vacations," explained Suzanne Slesin. *"But, all that changed rather dramatically about five years ago when we decided to build a small, economical house on a piece of land we had owned for years in Sag Harbor, New York. We took on the challenge of ordering a pre-fab house with a rusted corrugated steel exterior and a variegated dark wood plank interior from weeHouse, a Minneapolis, Minnesota-based company."* Of course, everything in the interior—from the art, to the furnishings, to the tableware—needed to be rethought. *"We started by collecting vintage pieces from the 1950s and 1960s by artisans who were based in Vallauris, a village known for its pottery in the South of France,"* said Slesin. *"Soon, we realized that we needed some everyday plates and bowls that would fit in nicely with the Arts and Crafts aesthetic, and would add a touch of lightness and prettiness to the earthy environment. Mottahedeh's simple and beautifully colored Leaf pattern stoneware, two bright majolica pieces, and a few strong Rookwood items would be right at home."*—Suzanne Slesin

PAGES 214–215 A field of daisies softens the rusted corrugated exterior of the pre-fab house that was designed by Geoffrey Warner of the Minneapolis, Minnesotta-based firm, Alchemy Architects for weeHouse.

PREVIOUS PAGES RIGHT A Classic Rookwood vase in red and black has been placed on a distressed metal table that was found in Lambertville, New Jersey. The rough-hewn walls act as a fitting background for the strong silhouette of the pottery.

OPPOSITE In the kitchen, a service of Leaf stoneware in Agate is handily stored on open, rolled black metal shelves. The two pitchers are by the French ceramicist, Robert Picault, who worked in Vallauris, France, in the 1950s.

RIGHT The table is set in the dining room with mugs, bowls, and plates in the Leaf pattern stoneware in Agate. A distinct outline of a leaf stands out against the gradient glaze of the larger pieces. On the wall is a framed folk-art collection of pencils, each of which is marked with a business in Upstate New York. The linen napkins are from Sferra.

LEFT A Leaf pasta bowl has been placed in the center of a table made by the French ceramicist Roger Capron, who worked in Vallauris in the 1950s. His ceramic-tiled tables with their burnt-in leaves gives a coincidental, but stylish nod to Mottahedeh's stoneware Leaf design.

OPPOSITE Mottahedeh's 12-inch square Rookwood pinecone tray, painted in a warm earth tone vellum glaze, complements the nature-themed table by Capron.

OPPOSITE The generously proportioned Grape leaf tureen and stand are reminiscent of the majolica pottery made in 18th-century English factories that reproduced fruits, vegetables, and animals. Now made in Italy, the majolica tureen can be used as a centerpiece on a table or a sideboard to serve cold food. Here, it stands on a Wrongwoods cabinet by Sebastian Wrong and Richard Woods for the English company Established & Sons.

RIGHT The green leaf majolica dish with its delicately carved vine handle was made in Italy and is the perfect vessel for candy, nuts, or keys. The transluscent green glaze accents the texture and veins in the leaves.

223

EXOTIC PATTERNS IN A TROPICAL PARADISE

"In Palm Beach where I have an interior design office, my husband Peter Wilson and I live at The Reef, a landmarked Postmodern masterpiece designed by the Florida-based architect Gene Lawrence in 1975. The building is white and all the furniture on the terraces has to be white so when I entertain outside, I like to have bright colors that don't fight with the architecture of the building." For a luncheon on a corner of the terrace that is framed by lush tropical greenery and a vase filled with Birds of Paradise blooms, the table is set with Barriera Corallina, designed by Tony Duquette. "For Duquette," added Hutton Wilkinson, "coral branches were like exploding fireworks." Sanders added that indoors, "I like to pair Mottahedeh's rather subdued and elegant Leaf china with an exuberantly colorful tablecloth and tropical flowers set into a vintage seashell to create 'a tropical fantasy.'" Being in Florida, Sanders added, "is about mixing as many colors together to create an exotic feeling that goes right along with enjoying the warm weather, being whimsical, and having fun."—Scott Sanders

PAGES 224–225 On Scott Sanders' terrace, the Mottahedeh Barriera Corallina pattern, with its raised branches of bright red coral, is offset against a white background. To complete the table setting, Sanders added colorful glasses, a series of brass candlesticks from Remains Lighting with orange candles, bamboo-handled flatware, large banana leaf–like placemats, and napkins by Kim Seybert. The table and chairs are by Richard Schultz for Knoll.

PREVIOUS PAGES RIGHT A pair of 8-inch-high monkey bookends in Mottahedeh's Creamware collection stand by a Barriera Corallina platter. The two ceramic vases are from France.

RIGHT The dining area, just off the kitchen, at one end of the long living room, opens up onto the terrace. The brass standing lamp by the Italian designer Tommaso Barbi dates from the 1970s, and a large canvas by the Taiwanese artist Yuh-Shioh Wong frame the dining table, which is set with plates and bowls in Mottahedeh's Leaf pattern stoneware in pale blue. The tablecloth is from Tessitura Toscana Telerie; the Dip-Dye napkins are by Kim Seybert; and the flatware is from Alain Saint-Joanis. The extravagant centerpiece of orchids is by Tom Mathieu, a florist in Palm Beach. The vintage chairs are from the 1970s.

229

OPPOSITE The blue silk hue of the Leaf stoneware service is perfect for this tropical table setting.

RIGHT Mottahedeh's colorful, 15½-inch-high cockatoos, reproductions of mid-18th-century Meissen originals, were inspired by the works of Joachim Kaendler, who studied animals and birds in the zoos and aviaries of his royal patron, Augustus III of Saxony and Poland. The originals date from 1736 to 1740. Birds are a very popular decorative element and can add a touch of whimsy to any room.

231

ELEGANT PORCELAINS COMPLETE AN OLD-WORLD FANTASY

Alex Papachristidis, the New York–based interior designer said, "I am by nature a classical decorator who loves timeless interiors." He sets his luxurious, and beautifully detailed tables in the Upper East Side apartment, in which he lives with his partner Scott Nelson and their Norwich terrier Cooper, with Mottahedeh pieces that he describes as, "the kind of china that feels timeless and is appropriate in my interiors as it has an old-world elegance that I love." Yet, Papachristidis also likes to mix traditional porcelain with more contemporary elements to give it a fresh and new look. His love of collecting objects, porcelain, and vermeil includes wonderful 18th-century Chinese porcelain, fruits and vegetables by the Glasgow, Scotland–born Lady Anne Gordon, and numerous fruit-laden trees in antique vintage brush pots by Vladimir Kanevsky, an Ukrainian-born artist. "I love looking at beautiful things," Papachristidis explained. "In your home, everything you use, touch, or eat off should be pretty."
—Alex Papachristidis

PAGES 232–233 Atop a chest of drawers in his atmospheric Manhattan living room, against a romantic background of Chinese wallpaper custom-made by New York's Gracie Studio, Alex Papachristidis artfully displays some of the objects that he loves to collect, including 18th-century Chinese Export porcelain, a porcelain cauliflower by Lady Anne Gordon, and a plum-laden tree in an antique vase by Vladimir Kanevsky, an Ukrainian-born artist.

PREVIOUS PAGES RIGHT In the dining room, a Mottahedeh tureen and stand in Chinoise Blue, a pattern derived from 18th-century Chinese Export porcelain, have been centered under an *églomisé* Chinoiserie painting. The pair of kumquat trees are by Vladimir Kanevsky. The walls have been upholstered in a wool felt with nail heads.

RIGHT "My love of nature is very important, and I love faux-bois," said Papachristidis who set the gilded tree-branch–like table in the living room with a Chinoise Blue tea service. The pattern has simple leaf and ribbon borders in gold, cobalt, and rust to create a subtle yet elegant effect. The coffee table plays well with the 22-karat gold accents in the china. "The blue in this pattern complements all the lavender tones that I have in the apartment," added Papachristidis. The flowers throughout are by Zezé.

PREVIOUS PAGES Setting a formal table is one of the interior designer's specialties. Papachristidis mixes two patterns—Chinoise Blue and Golden Butterfly on a table from Maison Jansen to create a more interesting tablescape. The hurricane lamps are made in Paris and the custom linens and organza placemats are made in Italy. All are from the designer's Everyday Elegance Collection. The cobalt, Chinese red, and 22-karat gold accents of the china are echoed in the salt cellars and *objets d'art*. Classic and gold-edged glassware are combined for this special occasion. The chalk-white painted chairs have been upholstered in a velvet from Carolina Irving Textiles.

OPPOSITE AND RIGHT The place setting brings together two classic Chinese Export patterns. The Chinoise Blue dinner plate is topped with a Golden Butterfly salad plate. A small square Chinoise Blue plate adds interest with its shape and is placed here for the amuse-bouche. The flatware, from Alain Saint-Joanis, in wood and gilded metal, is a perfect accompaniment to the luxurious porcelain. The beautiful geometric placemats and napkins are from Alex Papachristidis linens for the Everyday Elegance Collection. The raspberry detailing in the scalloped placemats is picked up in the colors of the Zezé flower arrangement. "I love the idea of slightly clashing my colors, as it makes the whole look so much richer and pretty," Papachristidis said.

OVERLEAF In the kitchen, with its classic New York view, Papachristidis has assembled a collection of blue-and-white porcelain, including Mottahedeh pieces that he has collected over time. A silver cabbage by Buccellatti, silver palm trees from Tiffany & Co., and silver animals and trays add to the glittery scene.

MOTTAHEDEH PATTERNS

In matters of taste, one person may look at our objects and decide that he or she doesn't like them at all, while another person may think they are the cat's meow. Our specialty is making accurate and beautiful reproductions of classic designs, and our main focus is making brilliant objects to use every day. A number of dinner plates and figurines are new creations, and have never been seen before, such as the Famille Rose presentation bowl, the Brighton Pavilion pair of birds, and the Ch'ing Garden dinner service. In my work life, I concentrate less on getting ahead and more about doing the best work we can so that we are worthy of people's confidence. A company can have fine products, but all aspects of the business have to be positive experiences for them; for instance, sufficient inventory and shipping on time. Getting a live person on the phone is not always possible, but it is our intention. People are social beings and we want those who call us to have a "human experience." We make decorative items that people don't necessarily need, but they want. Beauty is for everybody.

STARBURST MEDALLION
Tony Duquette, known as an "American Design Icon," designed these plates, featuring cut stone-like panels that have been painted in a playful way. The powerful colors make a bold statement and the gold gives the design a serious touch of elegance. Available in three colorways—Green Malachite, Blue Lapis Lazuli, and Red Tortoise. Starburst Medallion is a licensed product of Tony Duquette. **PAGES 188-189, 191, 192, 193, 200-201, 203**

TASSEL
This pattern is adapted from a dessert service in the Collection at the Winterthur Museum, Garden & Library. The original plate was manufactured at the Manufacture Le Vieux Paris between 1820 and 1836. The pattern shows a geometric green leaf design with tassels and liberal gold accents, and is a fine example of French opulence from the early 1800s. **PAGES 110, 111**

CHINOISE BLUE
This pattern is derived from the 18th-century Chinese Export porcelain that can be seen in several decorative arts museums. The simple leaf and ribbon borders in gold, cobalt, and rust create a subtle yet elegant effect. This service is equally appropriate in a boardroom, on a formal dinner table, or used in a more casual setting. **PAGES 57, 235, 236-237, 238-239, 240, 241**

BLUE CANTON
This pattern has been a favorite for centuries. Pagodas, bridges, and landscapes appear in finely shaded cobalt blues, recreating the design of the original Chinese Export wares. The most fashionable tables in the early American Republic were set with blue-and-white "Canton" or "Nanking" china, which were named for the great Chinese trading ports from which they came. Blue Canton is a licensed product of the Historic Charleston Foundation. **PAGES 3, 56, 101, 119, 120-121, 125, 156, 157, 158-159, 160, 204, 205, 242-243, BACK COVER**

BLUE SHÒU
Elements of the iconic Blue Canton pattern have been adapted to this new pattern, merging them into sleek modern shapes. The word Shòu, pronounced "show," is the Chinese word for longevity. The pine tree, a key element of the pattern, symbolizes endurance and long life. Blue Shòu is produced in cobalt on bright white porcelain and is a classic color pairing. **PAGES 156, 157**

PEACOCK
The cobalt blue lines that make up the feathers in the peacock tail are underlaid with a wash of green, turquoise, and other colors that are visually intriguing. Even though the motif includes a false gold for the sparkle, the pattern is microwavable and dishwasher safe. **PAGES 78, 79**

VIRGINIA BLUE

This pattern is a perfect example of the use of an original design to inspire a new and different creation. The dinner plate was part of Colonial Williamsburg's extensive collection, originally owned by the Beverley family. We thought this plate was interesting and lively, with its scalloped edge and linework painted in cobalt blue. The original design was deconstructed by enlarging the central bird and foliage motif and lifting it off the dinner plate to put it on the dessert plate. The dinner plate now has the original lacy border, but with a plain center. The cobalt blue color was then tipped toward a periwinkle or slightly purple hue and the plain background of the dessert and dinner, bread and butter plate, and cup and saucer became a pearlized ecru—a slightly yellow hue—giving it a light-catching sheen. We hope it will have the same longevity that its predecessor has enjoyed. It is a licensed product of Colonial Williamsburg. **PAGES 57, 144, 145**

MANDARIN BOUQUET

This pattern features a charming bouquet of flowers in a basket, also seen in an 18th-century Chinese Hong Bowl, *top*, surrounded by an undulating classic blue-and-white Fitzhugh border. George Washington's Cincinnati, *above*, is a similar plate design, with the difference being the center motif. Washington was the first President General of a society, whose mission was to recognize the honorable services of former French and American officers of the American Revolution. The society took its name from the ancient Lucius Quintus Cincinnatus, who was appointed dictator in time of crisis and, after defeating the enemies of the Roman Republic, returned to his farm, giving up all political and military power. In the center of the plate is the society's insignia: Fame holding aloft the American eagle. The service was purchased for Washington by General Henry Lee. It was produced and decorated in Canton, China, in 1784 and brought to America on the first United States ship to enter the China Trade. It is a licensed product of Winterthur Museum, Garden & Library **PAGES 99, 100, 101, 107, 116, 117**

SACRED BIRD & BUTTERFLY

This Chinese Export pattern, from about 1800, features an all-over design of motifs rendered with characteristic understatement and translucency in traditional Chinese orange and gold colors. The marriage of shape and design was a success and was reproduced thereafter in English china. Sacred Bird & Butterfly in blue is a colorway never seen before. It was launched at the time of this printing, in hues of translucent blue and silver, and banded in gold. They are licensed products of the Historic Charleston Foundation. **PAGES 56, 122, 123, 130, 131**

CHELSEA FEATHER

Chelsea Feather, a versatile and elegant design, is an updated and simplified version of a shape we have carried for many years. It is a replica of a design produced at the Chelsea Manufactory, one the earliest English factories, established around 1740 and merged in 1745 with another ceramics producer. The Chelsea factory is known for its animals, figurines, and botanical shapes, done in an elaborate painting style. The five patterns we have made in this shape are Chelsea Botanicals, Duke of Gloucester, Chelsea Birds, Chelsea Feather, and Chelsea Feather Turquoise. **COVER, BACK COVER, PAGES 44, 45**

CH'ING GARDEN

The 18th-century hand-painted Chinese wallpaper in the dining room of the Lightfoot House in Colonial Williamsburg, *second from the top*, was the inspiration for this exquisite pattern. The decoration incorporates blossoming trees, hanging baskets of flowers, and exotic birds. Chinese decorative arts, known as Chinoiserie, were first popular in the 18th century and continue to be today. This pattern is a licensed product of Colonial Williamsburg. **PAGES 38-39, 40, 41, 42, 43**

BLUE DRAGON
In China, the dragon became the symbol for the emperor during the Tang dynasty, bestowing good fortune and protection to the righteous. The period of the Emperor Kangxi (1622-1722) was one of the high points in the development of blue-and-white wares. This period inspired Mottahedeh's classic design.
PAGES 55, 152-153, 155, 164, 165

SWAN SERVICE
The original of the Swan Service was produced at Meissen, the first European porcelain factory, in Saxony, now a state in Germany. The first service of 2,200 pieces was commissioned in 1737 for Count Heinrich Brühl, the director of the Meissen factory. Former Vice President Nelson Rockefeller purchased some of the original plates and asked Mottahedeh to make dinnerware, as well as a tea service to match it.
PAGES 88-89

BARGELLO
This charming pattern has a contemporary vibrancy and versatility that belies its antique origins. The Bargello dinnerware is adapted from English porcelain from about 1810. Like the needlework for which it is named, it combines dashes of red, green, blue, yellow, orange, and magenta in a geometric patchwork enhanced by 22-karat gold lines. It is reminiscent of contemporary ikats or Southeast Asian–style textile designs. **PAGE 10**

WATERDANCE
The fish motifs in this pattern were taken from Chinese watercolor paintings on paper in the library at the Winterthur Museum, Garden & Library in Winterthur, Delaware. The transparent feel of the paintings was captured in the entirely different medium of ceramics. But images on paper do not always translate well to glassy ceramics as one's eye perceives them differently. Paper absorbs light and porcelains reflect light. I wanted to express the translucent nature of water captured in this watercolor. We then added touches of silvery mica to catch the light on the fish's scales. I was initially attracted to the lovely carp and then looked for other fish in the library that could work well on the serving pieces, whose shapes were designed for this pattern that is a licensed product of the Winterthur Museum, Garden & Library. **PAGES 86, 87, 128**

LACE
The decoration of this pattern is a series of fine lines that create a crisscross lace-like effect. The overall appearance is that of a simple solid. Our Lace pattern started off as three service plates in cobalt blue, rust red, and leaf green. Later it was developed into a dinner service in cobalt blue, which included serving bowls, rimmed soup plates, platters, oval-lobed trays, mugs, and dessert bowls. Over time, the pattern expanded to five different colors for all the pieces, along with sandwich trays and footed cake plates. The colors are pink, apple green, cornflower blue, leaf green, and cobalt. Dishwasher and microwave safe. Not stopping there, we created a multicolored butterfly to be used with all the Lace colorways. **PAGES 57, 70-71, 73, 74-75, 178-179, 181, 208-209, 211**

BARRIERA CORALINA
This uniquely beautiful pattern features ten-faceted plates with a necklace of hand-painted, raised red coral on the shoulder. The design was adapted from Tony Duquette's idea sketchbook in which he designed many hand-painted pieces for a coral dinner service. The pattern is available in gold, platinum, and red. Duquette was a movie set designer in the heyday of grand musical motion pictures and became the interior decorator for many Hollywood stars. His motto was "More is More." This pattern is a licensed product of Tony Duquette. **PAGES 151, 224-225, 227**

SYLVANAE
The name of this pattern is the Latin word for the goddesses of the forest. The beguiling woodland scene is an adaptation of a Zsolnay Porcelain Manufactory design that was first produced in the late 1800s in Pecs, Hungary. The swirling motif, on a generously sized plate, features three exotic birds and multicolored flora intertwined with leaves. The dessert plate is an exact reproduction. Microwave and dishwasher safe. **PAGES 76, 77**

IMPERIAL BLUE
Since the Ming Dynasty, imperial blue-and-white porcelains have been prized by collectors and connoisseurs around the world. Edged in 22-karat gold, this underglazed blue dinner service is based on a Chinese Export pattern that dates from about 1730. The elegant design features a central flowered medallion, continuous collar, floral sprays, and a crisscross band of blue in the center of the plate. It looks like a solid, but on closer inspection, it is a series of fine lines that create a lace-like effect. This pattern is a licensed product of Colonial Williamsburg. **PAGES 3, 73, 74, 142, 143**

LEAF
The Leaf pattern came about after a lot of homework. I looked at many early Korean and Chinese glazes as these are tried-and-true and still admired today. I saw a marvelous outline of a leaf fused onto a black plate in the style of raku. One could see all the detail in the linework. We decided to do something not done on today's stoneware: start with a reactive fluid glaze in a first firing and then fire a second time to fuse a skeleton leaf into the plate. The perfect leaf was selected during a walk in the woods, which is how we came up with the combination of a gradient glaze effect with the distinct outline of a leaf. The four colorways are Blue Haze, White Silk, Topaz, and Agate. **PAGES 51, 218, 219, 220, 228-229, 230**

PROSPERITY
This pattern originally was a very durable 18th-century Staffordshire salt-glazed stoneware with a grey-white body. The Prosperity dinner service Mottahedeh created replicates the fine reticulated surface of the plates but was captured with scanning and 3-D printing and produced in thin, bright white, high-fired porcelain. The rim is unglazed, stain-proof, and is dishwasher and microwave safe. Prosperity is a licensed product of Mount Vernon. **PAGES 46, 47, 97, 103, 104-105, 151, 206-207**

FAMILLE VERTE
The name of this pattern means "green family" in French. This group of porcelains, many of which were produced in China during the reign of Emperor Kangxi from 1662-1722, is characterized by decorations in shades of green. Our graceful design, with its goji berries and leaves, was inspired by porcelain in the Chinese Imperial Palace. Our entire dinner service and decorative objects were inspired by a small bowl in the collection of the Metropolitan Museum of Art, in New York. It was once owned by Augustus the Strong, Elector of Saxony and King of Poland. The porcelain used for the style is called a "grey body"—a porcelain clay or white body that has a large amount of iron in it, giving the fired piece a grey or bluish tone—because Chinese wares of the 1700s and later were made with this type of clay. It tones down the color of the decoration that is fired into it, giving it an authentic, softer look. If you turn over the plate you can see the true color more readily. Kaolin, a disintegrated granite, is the common yet essential ingredient that allows porcelain to be fired and melted at very high temperatures. The Chinese had access to clay that was high in iron. **PAGES 34-35, 36, 37**

CHELSEA BIRD
The porcelain factory that originally produced this china was among the first and most significant in England after the Europeans discovered that the secret to making porcelain was the addition of kaolin, disintegrated granite, to the clay. The Chelsea Manufactory was established in London in 1743. These pieces feature shapes common to Chinese Export, English, and Continental porcelain of the 18th century. The Chelsea Manufactory is known for its curvy and botanically inspired shapes. Chelsea's "disheveled" birds are attributed to James Giles, an independent porcelain decorator of high repute who worked for a number of well-known factories. Chelsea Bird is a licensed product of Colonial Williamsburg. **PAGES 133, 134-135, 136, 137, BACK COVER**

MERIAN
The development of the exceptional service is intertwined with the life of Maria Sybilla Merian, a botanical illustrator and unrecognized scientist who lived from 1646 to 1717. The spark of the design began when the Mottahedehs bought a rare and important plate featured in their authoritative book, *China for the West*. The Chinese plate was produced around 1734 using Merian's book, *Metomorphosis Insectorum Surinamenuim* that was published in Holland in 1705. Merian was studying and documenting the transformation of insects from pupal stages to full-grown insects when it was believed that insects materialized out of puddles. In many cases, the insects were depicted chewing on her artistically drawn plants. Since they only had the one plate as a reference for the polychrome dinner service, they went back to the original book and chose three compatible black-and-white line drawings to use as flower images and then had a skilled painter color them for the dessert plates. We also used the Chinese chain design and interior band of the porcelain plate. We owe a debt of gratitude to Francoise Susini for her exceptionally delicate and beautiful painting. A special feature of this work is that no two images are the same on the various pieces of this service. There are 25 different color screens and raised enamels. This pattern was discontinued because of the lack of ability to get the silkscreen color decorations produced, but our plan is to re-introduce it in honor of our 100th anniversary. **PAGES 14, 30, 31, 32, 33**

DUKE OF GLOUCESTER
When Colonial Williamsburg and Mottahedeh began working together in 1989, the first reproduction that was made was a small Royal Worcester platter in the Colonial Williamsburg collection, which was created in 1770 for the Duke of Gloucester, the brother of King George III of England. Thereafter, we made an exact reproduction of the full and singular antique service of this design, using historical Worcester shapes for the serving piece. Dan Melman, a shape designer, sculpted a tureen and stand using archival references for the effusive Rococo design. The items were cast by hand and decorated in Europe. Duke of Gloucester is a licensed product of Colonial Williamsburg. **PAGES 138-139, 140-141**

DUPAQUIER
This pattern, in shades of black, grey, and gold, are reproductions of the famed Jagd porcelain service produced at the DuPaquier factory in Vienna, Austria around 1730. The factory was the only other factory in Europe to compete with the Meissen factory in Saxony and was among the first to discover the secret of making porcelain that remained hidden from Westerners for hundreds of years. The DuPaquier reproductions include a set of four luncheon plates and a platter, which are decorated with grisaille forest animals and 22-karat gold. **PAGES 172-173, 174, 175**

EMMELINE

This pattern is a blend of modern and old-world designs. The blue-and-white floral motifs were reproduced from Chinese Export porcelain from around 1755, and was a new look for the factories at the time. Drawings were sent to China to instruct artists in European style decoration to accommodate the changing tastes of the West. One French merchant wrote, "send no more dragons but let us have flowers instead." Emmeline's plate shapes are contemporary, while the styling is on a French white body, a departure from the classic Chinese grey body porcelain. **PAGES 161, 162-163**

BLUE TORQUAY

The elegant resort town of Torquay, which clings to the coast of Devon in southern England, is renowned for its mild climate and its abundant marine life. The shells and entwined sea grasses inspired the Swansea potters who flourished there between 1764 and 1846. The Blue Torquay English transferware pattern was created around 1820 and was developed with the Winterthur Museum, Garden & Library. The dinner service was originally produced by Burgess and Leigh in Stoke-on-Trent, with the exacting production of inking a zinc plate, making a transfer onto tissue paper, and applying the paper to bisque stoneware. This method was a precurser to the waterslide lithography used today. Blue Torquay is a licensed product of the Winterthur Museum, Garden & Library. **PAGES 83, 114, 115**

GOLDEN BUTTERFLY

The original pattern of this distinguished dinner service was made in China for the East India Company during the reign of the Qianlong Emperor (1736-1795). The service was developed in collaboration between Nelson Rockefeller, former Vice President of the United States, and the Mottahedehs. While the pattern has been named Golden Butterfly, we believe that the design actually shows a moth with outstretched wings on a blue starry field depicting night, juxtaposed with birds soaring in a light-filled sky. The circle of the plate symbolizes the cycle of day and night. **PAGES 238-239, 240, 241**

TOBACCO LEAF

This extravagant design was originally made in China, probably for export to the Portuguese and Brazilian markets. Of all the 18th-century dinner patterns, this was the most highly prized. A small phoenix bird perches on the leaves of the flowering *Nicotiana*, or Tobacco plant. Twenty-seven colors and 22-karat gold make up the pattern that is based on an original in the Metropolitan Museum of Art, in New York. This design, one of the longest running Mottahedeh patterns, continues to be very popular today, proving that good design is timeless. **BACK OF FRONT ENDPAPERS, PAGES 1, 17, 57, 194-195, 197, 198, 199, 208-209, 211, 212-213, BACK COVER**

PALMA

Palma is a reproduction of a dinner service from about 1840, which was designed by Fyodor Solntsev, the great Russian art historian, who painted interiors for cathedrals and designed much of the Kremlin under the patronage of Tsar Nicolas I. The lavish decoration incorporates the elements of a plate owned by Tsar Alexei Mikhailovich, which dates to 1667, and was inspired by the domes of the magnificent mosques in Istanbul, Turkey. The center of the plate is reminiscent of Celtic patterns. Truly universal in its theme, this historic design seems contemporary—the mark of excellent design. **PAGES 151, 182, 183, 184-185, BACK COVER**

WENDY'S COOKIE RECIPES

MARZIPAN SLICES

This is my variation of the famous Swedish Princess Cake—a crisp, buttery cookie overlaid with soft marzipan filling, then studded with pearl sugar, and sliced almonds, toasted in the oven for added crunch.
Yield: 42 to 48 bars

INGREDIENTS
2¼ cups sifted all-purpose flour
½ tsp double acting baking powder
¼ tsp salt
6 ounces (1½ sticks) butter
2 tsp vanilla extract
⅔ cup sugar
1 egg
One 7 ounce tube of almond paste (marzipan), cut into small pieces
1 egg white
1 tsp almond extract
Sliced almonds
Pearl sugar

DIRECTIONS
Preheat oven to 375°F.
Sift together flour, baking powder, and salt. Set aside. In the large bowl of an electric mixer, cream the butter. Add the vanilla and sugar, and beat well. Beat in the egg. On the lowest speed, add the sifted dry ingredients, scraping the bowl with a rubber spatula and beating until the dry ingredients are thoroughly incorporated. Turn out onto a lightly floured board. Shape into a ball and cut into four equal parts. Working on the board with your fingertips, flour them if the dough sticks, work each piece into a roll about 12 inches long and 1-inch in diameter.
Place the rolls crosswise on a large unbuttered cookie sheet 14 by 16 inches, leaving 2 to 3 inches of space between them. The rolls will spread out quite a bit. Make a narrow, shallow trench down the length of each roll by pressing gently with a fingertip. Leaving a little space at the ends, work the full length in one direction, and then work in the opposite direction.
In a food processor, blend the almond paste with the egg white and almond extract until almost smooth. Using a small spoon, fill all the trenches, mounding the marzipan paste slightly. Sprinkle pearl sugar intermittently along the marzipan mounds. Press sliced almonds into the marzipan and pearl sugar.
Bake for about 25 minutes until the cookies are sand-colored on top and golden brown around the edges, reversing the position of the pan during baking to ensure an even color and so the almond slices are brown on the edges. When cool, cut into long bars crosswise with a large, flat, and very sharp knife. Serve or store airtight for two weeks in the freezer.

ALMOND FLAVOR THUMBPRINTS

"The people's #1 choice" at Mottahedeh tabletop markets and gatherings. I often double the recipe, as this is a crowd pleaser.
Yield: 42 to 48 cookies

INGREDIENTS
2¾ cups flour
½ cup sugar
8 ounces (2 sticks) sweet butter
1 yolk from extra-large egg
½ tsp almond extract
¼ tsp salt
½ cup each of strawberry, apricot, or blackberry jam (seedless)

Glaze (make while the cookies are baking)
1 cup confectioners sugar mixed with 2 tbs boiling water and 1 tsp almond extract, stirred until smooth. It should flow, but not be runny.

DIRECTIONS
Preheat oven to 375°F.
Using an electric mixer, cream the butter with the sugar, egg yolk, salt, and almond extract until smooth and well-combined. On low speed, add the flour in three parts and combine well. Dough should be crumbly and just barely hold together.
Line a baking sheet (double thickness or two metal sheets on top of each other) with light-colored parchment paper. Roll the dough into walnut-size balls.
Space the balls 1 inch apart on the baking sheet. Make an indentation in each with your thumb. Fill the indentations with your favorite jam, but don't fill above the dough level.
Bake for 8 to 12 minutes, until golden. It helps to reverse the cookie sheets front to back halfway through baking for even doneness.
Upon removing baking sheets from the oven, brush the hot cookies with the confectioners sugar glaze. This will drip over the sides.
When completed, transfer the cookies to a rack to dry and let sit for a few hours or overnight.
Place in an airtight container and freeze if not serving right away. Cookies can be frozen and stored for a month or more. If you are a skilled baker, these take about 45 minutes for preparation time from start to finish.
Note:
1. For lemon lovers, substitute lemon extract for the almond extract and use lemon curd instead of jam.
2. I usually triple or quadruple the batch so I am not sure if you need one large baking sheet or two.

CHOCOLATE WALNUT CHERRY JUMBLES

These cookies are mocha, bittersweet, chewy, and have a bright note contributed by the cherries.
Yield: 36 cookies

INGREDIENTS
2 ounces (2 squares) unsweetened chocolate
6 ounces (6 squares) semisweet chocolate
2 tbs butter
¼ cup sifted all-purpose flour
¼ tsp double-acting baking powder
⅛ tsp salt
2 eggs
¾ cup sugar
1 tsp instant coffee
1 tsp vanilla extract
6 ounces (1 cup) white chocolate morsels
8 ounces (2¼ cups) walnuts or pecans, broken into medium pieces
1 cup dried cherries

DIRECTIONS
Preheat oven to 325°F.
Adjust an oven rack one-third down, cut aluminum foil to fit cookie sheets, and spray with cooking oil.
In the top of a small double boiler over hot water over moderate heat, melt the unsweetened and semisweet chocolates and the butter. Set aside to cool completely.
Sift together the flour, baking powder, and salt. Set aside.
In the small bowl of an electric mixer beat the eggs, sugar, coffee, and vanilla at high speed for 1 to 2 minutes. On low speed, add the cooled chocolate mixture and finally the sifted dry ingredients, scraping the bowl with a rubber spatula to keep the mixture smooth, and beating until only blended. Stir in the white chocolate morsels and nuts.
Drop by heaping teaspoonfuls 1 inch apart (cookies barely spread) on the aluminum foil. Slide a cookie sheet under the foil.
Bake 10 to 12 minutes, reversing the position of the cookie sheet if necessary during baking to ensure even browning. Do not overbake. It is hard to tell when these are done because they are so dark. Touch the cookie with your finger and when the sheen is off the surface, it is cooked. With a wide metal spatula remove cookies to cool on a rack.

PISTACHIO SABLÉS

Sablé is a French version of shortbread, adding egg yolks and omitting cornstarch. This gives it a less crumbly, more durable texture, sometimes referred to as a sandy texture. Sablé is the word for sand in French.
Yield: 48 cookies

INGREDIENTS
2½ cups unbleached all-purpose flour
8 ounces (2 sticks) cold, salted butter, cut into little pieces
⅔ cup sugar
2 egg yolks
1 tsp vanilla extract
½ cup finely ground, roasted, and salted pistachio nuts
½ tsp salt
⅓ cup green sanding sugar
1 egg, beaten

DIRECTIONS
Preheat oven to 350°F.
In a large food processor, add flour, salt, sugar, egg yolks, and vanilla in the order listed above. Blend all until uniform in consistency.
Add the butter pieces to the mixture and blend until the dough is smooth. Divide the dough into two equal parts. On a 12-inch piece of waxed paper, shape a portion of dough into cylinders about 1½ inches in diameter. Repeat with the second portion of dough.
Combine the ground nuts and the green sanding sugar together. On another 12-inch piece of waxed paper, generously sprinkle the nuts and the green sanding sugar about three times the width of the cylinder. Brush the logs with the beaten egg. Place the cylinder on the sugar and roll back and forth to press the sugar evenly into the surface all the way around.
Place the sugared cylinder back on the first piece of waxed paper, roll the waxed paper tightly over it to form a smooth even package. Tuck the waxed paper ends in to close the package and put it in the freezer until it becomes solid. Repeat the process with the second piece of dough. Freezing allows you to slice the cylinder into cookie rounds so they will hold their shape. (I often leave it overnight or even a few days and thaw it just slightly). I use an empty paper towel roll and slide the cylinder into it to keep a more even shape of the dough while if freezes.
When you are ready to bake, unwrap the first cylinder, slice it into ⅓-inch-thick rounds and place them 1½-inches apart on a parchment-lined cookie sheet. Put into the middle of the oven while still cold and partially frozen to help them keep their shape as they bake. Bake for 12 to 16 minutes, until golden in the middle. Remove to a cooling rack.

OATMEAL LACE AND SPICE COOKIES

Elegant with a spicy twist of flavor, this cookie is one of my favorites.
Yield: 32 cookies

INGREDIENTS
¼ cup sifted all-purpose flour
½ tsp salt
¼ tsp baking soda
½ tsp cinnamon
1 tsp powdered ginger
½ tsp nutmeg
4 ounces (1 stick) butter at room temperature
¼ cup granulated sugar
½ cup firmly packed brown sugar
1 egg
1 cup old-fashioned (not instant) oatmeal
¾ cup almonds, finely chopped
2 cups semi-sweet chocolate morsels or melting chocolate
¼ cup heavy cream

DIRECTIONS
Preheat oven to 350°F.
Line cookie sheets with parchment paper.
Combine the first 6 dry ingredients and set aside. In a small bowl, with an electric mixer, beat sugars with the butter and the egg, then beat in the flour mixture. On the lowest speed, add the oatmeal, then almonds, scraping until incorporated. With a demitasse spoon, drop the mixture onto the baking sheet, leaving 3 inches between each mound. Repeatedly dipping the spoon in water, flatten each mound until it is thin and about 1½ inches in diameter. Bake for 15 minutes, until brown. Reverse the pans halfway through to ensure even baking. Remove from the oven, allow the cookies to cool until stiff. Carefully peel off the parchment. Turn the cookies over, match up the sizes to make an even sandwich.
Fill a heat-proof glass cup with 1 cup of chocolate morsels. Pour heavy cream over the morsels until it reaches the top layer of morsels, but doesn't cover them. Microwave for 1 minute on high. Remove and stir until the chocolate is smooth and blended and a little bit pourable. Place a small dollop of chocolate on one half of the cookies and cover the cookie with its matched pair to make a sandwich. The bumpy side of the cookie should be on the outside. When you have completed making the sandwiches, let the chocolate harden. Repeat the chocolate melting in a clean cup as above. You may reheat leftover chocolate but for no longer than 1 minute or it will burn. Dip the edge of your sandwich cookie in the melted chocolate and place on parchment paper or a cooling rack.

TRIPLE NUT PECAN COOKIES

This recipe is mostly nuts and the cookies are not overly sweet. The addition of coffee gives them a deeper flavor.
Yield: 22 cookies

INGREDIENTS
½ cup pecans, ⅓ cup walnuts, ⅓ cup almonds
4 ounces (1 stick) butter
½ tsp vanilla extract
½ tsp salt
¼ cup sugar
1½ tsps prepared coffee, water, or brandy
1 cup sifted all-purpose flour
22 pecan halves

DIRECTIONS
Preheat oven to 375°F.
Grind the nuts in a food processor along with the sugar and salt until fine. Set aside. In the small bowl of an electric mixer cream the butter. Stir in the vanilla. Beat in the coffee, water, or brandy. On the lowest speed, gradually add the flour. Scrape the bowl with a rubber spatula and beat until smooth. Add the ground nuts and beat until incorporated. Remove from mixer and place on wax paper. Flatten slightly, wrap, and refrigerate or freeze briefly until firm enough to handle.
Adjust oven rack one-third down.
Remove chilled dough from refrigerator or freezer and cut into 22 equal pieces.
Roll each piece into a ball. Place 1½ inches apart on an ungreased cookie sheet. Press a pecan half firmly into the top of each cookie, flattening it slightly.
Bake in a preheated oven for 18 to 20 minutes, until golden, reversing position of cookie sheet if necessary to ensure even browning.
With a metal spatula, transfer cookies to a rack to cool thoroughly.

SURPRISINGLY MINTY CHOCOLATE SANDWICHES

For a cookie recipe I was making, I forgot to get the specified peppermint. Necessity is the mother of invention, so searching around, I found a tin of Altoids and ground them up with a mortar and pestle. I added ground almonds to make the cookies more crisp. A surprisingly delicious new treat was created. Use black cocoa powder, which is what goes into Oreos. Who doesn't like an Oreo cookie?
Yield: 42 cookies

INGREDIENTS
4 ounces bittersweet chocolate
1½ cups finely ground almonds
1 cup sugar
⅓ cup black cocoa powder
1¾ cup flour
½ tsp baking powder
½ tsp baking soda
4 tbs ground Altoids (I use a mortar and pestle)
4 ounces (1 stick) butter, at room temperature
1 extra large egg
1 tbs vanilla extract
1 tsp mint extract
½ cup white chocolate (for filling)

DIRECTIONS
Preheat oven to 350°F.
In a food processor, grind until fine: bittersweet chocolate, ground almonds, sugar, and cocoa powder. Add and process flour, baking powder, baking soda and ground Altoids. Cream together in a small bowl the butter, egg, vanilla and mint extract. Stir dry ingredients into the butter mixture until incorporated. Form mixture into two cylinders, rolling them between waxed paper. Fold over the ends of the waxed paper and lay the cylinders in the freezer to harden. When frozen, take each cylinder out, unwrap it and, with a sharp knife, slice into thin disks. Put on cookie sheet lined with parchment ½ inch apart. Bake for 8 minutes.
When cookies are cooled, melt the white chocolate in the microwave for 1 minute and stir until smooth. Spread a small spoonful of white chocolate on each round and cover with another cookie to make a sandwich. Let stand until the chocolate is stiff. Pack in an airtight container.

GOLDEN SHORTBREAD

One of my favorites. It has a tender texture. Its buttery flavor melts in your mouth.
Yield: 36 cookies

INGREDIENTS
1 cup all-purpose flour
1 cup cornstarch
1 cup confectioners sugar
8 ounces (2 sticks) salted, very cold butter, cut into small pieces
3 or 4 drops yellow food coloring
Gold-colored sanding sugar

DIRECTIONS
Preheat oven to 325°F.
Add first 5 ingredients to a large food processor in the order listed above.
Add the food coloring so it will be blended into the dough. Process until all ingredients are blended and pull away from the sides to form a ball. Remove the dough from the processor. Cut into two equal pieces. On a 12-inch piece of waxed paper, form the dough into an oblong cylinder. Use both hands and roll the dough gently back and forth until it is 10 or 11 inches long and 1½ inches in diameter. On another 12-inch piece of waxed paper, generously sprinkle the gold-colored sanding sugar about three times the width of the cylinder. Place the cylinder on the sugar and roll back and forth to press the sugar evenly into the surface of the dough all the way around.
Place the sugared cylinder back on the first piece of waxed paper, roll the paper tightly over it to form a smooth even package. Tuck the waxed paper ends in to close the package and put it in the freezer until it becomes solid. Repeat the process with the second piece of dough. Freezing will allow you to slice the cylinder into cookie rounds. (I often leave it overnight or even for a few days and thaw it just slightly).
I use an empty paper towel roll and slide the cylinder into it to keep a more even shape while the dough freezes.
When you are ready to bake, unwrap one cylinder at a time, slice into ½-inch-thick rounds, and place 1½ inches apart on a parchment-lined cookie sheet. They should go into the oven while still cold and partially frozen. This will help the cookies to keep their shape. Bake for 12 to 16 minutes, until golden in the middle. Keep a good eye on the baking. These are very delicate and go from really good to overcooked in a flash.
Remove to a cooling rack.

DATE WALNUT BARS

A health bar disguised as a cookie, a very good-for-you confection. You can make this with a bowl and a spoon. It has plenty of crunch.
Yield: 24 bars

INGREDIENTS
1 cup all-purpose flour
¼ tsp baking powder
⅛ tsp salt
4 ounces (1 stick) melted butter
1 cup sugar
2 eggs
16 ounces (2 cups) pitted dates, coarsely cut
7 ounces (2 cups) walnut halves or broken pieces
Confectioners sugar

DIRECTIONS
Preheat oven to 350°F.
Adjust rack to center of oven. Line a shallow 9 x 13-inch jelly roll pan with a piece of aluminum foil long enough to cover the bottom and sides. Press the foil to mold it into place without tearing it. Brush the bottom and sides with very soft or melted butter. Set aside.
Stir together flour, baking powder, and salt. Set aside. In large bowl beat the melted butter and sugar with a spoon. Add the eggs and beat to them to mix. Add the sifted dry ingredients, beating only until incorporated. Mix in the dates and nuts. I usually increase the nuts and dates so the cookies barely hold together.
Spread this thick batter as smoothly as possible in the prepared pan, pressing it into place with the back of a large spoon, it will be stiff and lumpy. Fill in any holes. Bake for 35 minutes or until the top is a light golden brown. Remove from oven. Let cool in the pan on a rack for about 10 minutes. Place a cookie sheet over the top and invert again to cool completely.
Transfer to a cutting board. Use a ruler and toothpicks to mark even pieces. Cut into 24 bars with a long, thin, very sharp or finely serrated knife.
Sift confectioners sugar generously over the tops. These can be stored in an airtight container in the freezer for up to two months.

ACKNOWLEDGMENTS

From centuries past to today's tables, Mottahedeh's collection emerges as a testament to continuity. But no organization that has withstood the test of time can be sustained by one person. In the case of Mottahedeh & Co, Inc., it has had the benefit of the loving care, hard work, and special talents of too many people to count. You know who you are. I extend my gratitude to all of you. Please accept this acknowledgement as a heartfelt *THANK YOU*.

I have been with Mottahedeh for only 31 years of this long journey. I have always felt that our story is about the team and not purely about the Mottahedehs or about me.

A special thank-you goes to Paul Wojcik, Mottahedeh's Chief Visual Officer, who used his considerable talents to conceive, with our partnership, the concept, table displays, and styling of most of the settings in this book. Paul has the special ability to make friends with everybody and spread good cheer in all situations, including the most challenging ones. We had many a day of laughter mixed with hard work in producing these images.

We would not be able to produce these designs without the excellent abilities of some of the best factories worldwide—our friends who have gone the extra mile to make these designs a reality under all circumstances. Thank you to Pointed Leaf Press: to its publisher and editorial director, Suzanne Slesin, who brings many years of experience developing visual biographies in the worlds of design, architecture, and fashion; to Frederico Farina, the creative director who designed and made this book look as beautiful as it is; and to Julian Cosma, the editorial assistant, who kept us all on track; to Antoine Bootz, a masterful photographer whose work with light enhances the fine detail of any scene; to Carolyn Sollis, a respected editor and journalist, with more than 25 years of expertise in the field of home furnishings, interior design, and public relations. She assisted us in writing, cataloging, and organizing the many, many items in this work.

Thanks go to my husband Grant and family, including Miles, who have taken this journey with love and support. Dana Morand and Lauren Wei, our daughters, who put their skills to painting some spectacular cookies to illustrate our iconic patterns that they know so well. Last, we cannot forget the interior designers, architects, retailers, and event planners who have included our objects and dinnerware in their splendid interiors for both simple and special days.

—**Wendy Kvalheim**, January 2024

INDEX

Achille Castiglioni for Alessi, 192
Adamo, David, 182
Addington, Beverly, 94
Aitken, John, 97
Alain Saint-Joanis, 40, 51, 77, 78, 212, 228, 241
Alchemy Architects for weeHouse, Minneapolis, Minnesota, 216
Alhambra canape plates, 187
Alhambra Palace, Granada, Spain, 187
Almack, Colin, 42
Altman, Harold, 20
Apthorp building, New York, New York, 168, 171
Auburn, Maine, 68, 78
Audubon, James, 42
Augustus III of Saxony and Poland, 231
Ayres, John, 15
B&B Italia, 182
Baccarat, 32, 36
   Montaigne Optic pattern, 32, 36
Baha'i, 13, 15, 20, 60, 68
   "Tablet of Ahmad," 24
Baha'i Gardens, Akko, Israel, 68
Baker Furniture Stately Homes Collection, 28
Barbi, Tommaso, 228
Bargello dinnerware, 256
Barriera Corallina, 152, 226, 228
Beaver Furniture, Yorkshire, England, 42
Betbeze, Anna, 192
Beverley family, 144
Beverley, Robert, 132
Bianco Dolomite marble, 168
Bird Creamware tureen, 129, 147
Blandfield, Virginia, 132
Blue Canton, 54, 98, 118, 120, 156, 161, 205, 256
Blue Dragon, 54, 152, 164
Blue Hot Island glass vases, 68
Blue Shòu, 156
Blue Torquay pattern, 83, 114
Bonetti, Mattia, 192
Boston, Massachusetts, 36, 83
Boston Harbor bowl, 83
Boulanger, Graciela Rodo, 51
Brighton Pavilion, bird figurine, 134
Brown, Melissa, 212
Brühl, Count Heinrich, von, 88
Bruton Parish Episcopal Church, Williamsburg, Virginia, 132
Buatta, Mario, 196, 199
Buccellati, 31, 32, 241
Burgess and Leigh, 114
Butterfly Lace dessert plates, 182
Canton, China, 98, 118
Capron, Roger, 220
Carolina Irving Textiles, 241
Carp tureen, 87
Caspari placemats, 205
Chadduck, Heather, 142, 147
Chadwick, Lynn, 171
Charleston, South Carolina, 118, 123, 124
Chatsworth House, Derbyshire, England, 175, 187
Chelsea Birds pattern, 45, 134, 256
Chelsea Botanicals pattern, 45, 91
Chelsea Feather pattern, 45, 256
Chelsea Lettuce tureen, 256
Chelsea Physic Garden (Apothecaries' Garden), 91
Chelsea Porcelain Manufactory, 45, 256
Ch'ien Lung bowl, 26, 28
China for the West, 15
Chinese Chippendale, Baker Furniture's Stately Homes of England Collection, 28, 108
Chinese Export, 40, 98, 101, 108, 118, 131, 132, 199, 236, 241
Ch'ing Garden pattern, 40, 42
Chinoise Blue, 54, 236, 241
Christie's, 15
Cincinnati, Ohio, 51
Cincinnati service, 98, 101
Colonial Williamsburg, Williamsburg, Virginia, 40, 42, 93, 97, 132, 134, 137, 142, 256
   Lightfoot House, 134
   Nelson-Galt House, 97, 134
   Williamsburg Designer in Residence project, 142, 148
Cook, James, 78
Coral Torquay, 114
Cornflower Lace pattern, 46
Councill Contract, 36

Creamware collection, 68, 102, 147, 148, 228
Creamware, latticework urns, 97
Danceflower, 16, 20
DeMesse, Kristen, 106
De Roy, 83
Declaration of Independence, 134
Delft china, 154
Design AFI, 124
Diplomatic Service pattern, 94
Divina vase, 199
Dolphin candlesticks, 68
Dolphin-shell centerpiece, 68
du Pont, Henry Francis, 92, 106, 108, 111, 114
du Pont, Ruth Wales, 108
Duke of Gloucester pattern, 45, 132
DuPaquier, Vienna, Austria, 175
Duquette, Tony, 152, 192
East Hampton, New York, 152, 154
East India Company, England, 132
Eek, Piet Hein, 212
Eerdmans, Emily Evans, 196, 199
Eerdmans New York, 196
Einstein, Albert, 20
Eliot, Maine, 60, 83
Emmeline pattern, 161
Established & Sons, 223
Evergreen Place, Teaneck, New Jersey, 13
Everyday Elegance, 152, 182, 205, 241
Famille Verte pattern, 36
Fishman, Louise, 182
Fitzhugh borders, 94, 101, 117, 148
Fleuren, Alexandre, 124
Food Network, 52
Ford, Tom, 192
From Drawing Board to Dinner Table, 13, 52
Frothingham, James, 97
Fulbright scholarship, 175
Gabriel luncheon plate, 54
Galt family, Williamsburg, Virginia, 134
Garouste, Elisabeth, 192
Georg Jensen, 32
Gibbs and Channing, shipping firm, 118
Glasgow, Scotland, 234
Glittery Hydrangea placemats, 182
Golden Butterfly, 18, 241
Goodwin, W.A.R., 132
Gracie Studio, 16, 236
Grape Leaf tureen, 223
Greek Key pattern, 93
Greek Revival, 196
Green Acre Baha'í School, Eliot, Maine, 60
Green Torquay, 114
Gusler, Liza, 192
Hanscom, Samuel, Jr., 83
Hanscom Shipyard, Eliot Maine, 83
Harwood, Alison, 118
Heilmann, Mary, 192
Hepplewhite design, 36 120, 123
Hickory Chair Furniture Company, 36
Historic Charleston Foundation, Charleston, South Carolina, 93, 118, 123, 124, 131
HMS Endeavour, 78
Hoffman, Susan, 94
Hong bowl, 97, 101, 106, 108, 117
Houston, Katherine, 36
Howard, David, 15
Iatesta, David, 156
Imperial Blue pattern, 132, 142, 256
Innis, Callum, 175
Janus et Cie, 182
Jefferson, Thomas, 132
John Rosselli & Associates, 156
Johnson Atelier, Hamilton, New Jersey, 16, 20
Kaendler, Johann Joachim, 187, 231
Kangxi, Emperor, China 152
Kangxi period, China, 18
Kanevsky, Vladimir, 234, 236
Kartell, 182
King George III, 91, 132, 137
King, Judy, 68
Kittery, Maine, 60, 64, 87
Kvalheim, Dana, 78, 256
Kvalheim, Grant, 13, 20, 28

INDEX

Kvalheim, Laura, 256
Kvalheim, Miles, 256
Kohler, 42
Kremlin, Moscow, Russia, 182
Kremlin Service pattern, 182
L. & J.G. Stickley, 51, 68
    Iribe chair, 68
Lace pattern, 73, 77
Lace Tea for Two, 46, 182
Lalique, 20
Lambertville, New Jersey, 219
LaPaglia, Alphonse, 32
Larson, Natalie, 123
Lawrence, Gene, 226
Leaf Blue Haze pattern, 51
Leaf pattern stoneware, 216, 219, 220, 228, 231
Lee, Henry, 98
Leipold International, ceramic printing, 87
Levingold goblets, 142
Lexington pattern, 161, 199
London, England, 91, 132, 256
Long, Grahame, 118
Longton cookie plate, 54
Lorca Fabrics, 199
Lyons, Elizabeth, 161
Madeira, Portugal, 32, 36
Maison Jansen, 241
Malachite pattern, 205
Mandarin Bouquet pattern, 101, 117
Manlius, New York, 68
Mann, David, 180, 190
Mario Bellini for Cassina, 182
    Cab chairs, 182
Mario Luca Giusti, 152
Masullo, Andrew, 161
Match pewter, 142
Mathieu, Tom, 228
Maui, Hawaii, 68
Maynard, Jim, 175
Meissen, 88, 175, 187, 231
    Swan Service, 88
Melman, Dan, 137
Melon tureen, 256
Merian dinner service, 15, 20, 28, 31, 32
Merian, Maria Sybilla, 31
Metropolitan Museum of Art, New York, New York, 15, 18, 28, 32, 91
Milbert, A.J., 83
Milestone series, 51
Millennium bowl, 18, 20, 24
Ming plate, 28
    Palace Blue, 28
Monroe, James, 20
Monteith Bowl, 18
Montgomery, Paul, 134
    "Regency Views," 134
Morand, Kelsey Corinne, 1
Moretti, 192
Moser Glassware, 20
Mosse, Richard, 164
Mottahedeh, Mildred, 13, 15, 24, 28, 31, 118, 132, 256
Mottahedeh, Rafi, 13, 15, 31, 118
Mount Vernon, Virginia, 46, 93, 94, 97, 102, 108
    Bull's Eye Room, 102
    Garden House, 94
    New Room, 97
    The Mansion at Mount Vernon, 94
Mount Vernon Ladies Association, 94
Murano glass, 20, 124
Murano, Italy, 68
    Crystal, 124
    Glass, 20
Musée des Arts Décoratifs, Paris, France, 128, 147
Nathaniel Russell House, Charleston, South Carolina, 97, 118, 120, 123
    Withdrawing room, 120
National Museum of Ancient Art, Lisbon, 45
National Trust Presentation bowl, 98, 256
Nelson, Scott, 234
Nelson-Galt House, Williamsburg, Virginia, 97, 134, 256
New York, New York, 15, 18, 20, 171, 202, 210, 241
New York Gift Building, New York, New York, 18
New York Tabletop Show, New York, New York, 54
Nichols, Maria Longworth, 51

Nievera, Mario, 202, 205
Noble Stag tureen, 175
Nutleaf pattern, 91
Oakes, Lucinda, 199
Odiot, cutlery, 32
Palm Beach, Florida, 152, 154, 168, 180, 199, 226
Palma, 152, 182, 256
Papachristidis, Alex, 182, 205, 234, 236, 241
Paris, France, 128, 147, 192, 241, 256
Parisi, Ico, 232
Park Designs, 142
Peacock pattern, 78
Peale, Charles Wilson, 97
Peale, Rembrandt, 97
Pelzer, Cornelia, 118
Peter the Great, 182
Picault, Robert, 219
Pietra Dura design, 26, 192
Pont aux Choux, 128, 147
Porcelain, 12, 15, 16, 20, 28, 31, 32, 36, 46, 52, 73, 87, 88, 91, 94, 101, 106, 108, 114, 118, 120, 131, 132, 134, 147, 150, 156, 171, 175, 187, 205, 234, 236, 241, 256
Portsmouth, New Hampshire, 60, 83
Post, Jennifer, 168, 171, 175
Pratt Institute of Art, Brooklyn, New York, 20
Prince, Oliver Hillhouse, 111
Prince William Henry, Duke of Gloucester, 132, 137
Princeton, New Jersey, 16, 18, 20, 60
Princeton University, Princeton, New Jersey, 20
Prosperity dinner service, 46, 64, 94, 97, 102, 152, 205
Qalam, Mishkin, 24
Qing Dynasty, 108, 171
Radiate placemats, 182
Rahn, Wendy, 77, 78
Raku, 51
Ralph Pucci, 161
Ray, Susie, 91
Reagan bowl, 18
Reagan Monteith bowl, 18
Reagan, Nancy, 18
Reagan, Ronald, 18
Red Tortoise colorway, 192
Remains Lighting, 228
Repton, Humphrey, 134
Revolutionary War, 20, 108, 118, 132
Richard Schultz for Knoll, 228
Robert Haviland & C. Parlon, 161, 199
Rockefeller, Abby Aldrich, 132
Rockefeller, John D., Jr., 132
Rockefeller, Nelson, 15, 64, 88, 256
Rockefeller reproduction dinner plate, 18
Rookwood, 51, 171, 212, 216, 219
    Art Pottery, 51
    Classic vase, 171, 219
    Orion bowls, 51
    Pinewood tray, 220
    Sung Vase, 152, 171
Rowan, Carol, 73
Rowe, William Hutchinson, 83
Royal Navy, England, 78
Royal Worcester platter, 137
Russell, Nathaniel, 118, 120
Sacred Bird & Butterfly pattern, 54, 118, 123, 131
Sag Harbor, New York, 216
Sanders, Scott, 154, 156, 226, 228
Schumacher, 144, 148
    Dandrige Damask, 144
    Jakarta Linen Print, 148
Scott Sanders LLC, 164
Seletti, 212
    Hybrid glassware, 212
Sergio Asti for Knoll, 212
Seybert, Kim, 182, 228
Sferra, 182, 219
Shang vase, 131
Sharon, Russell, 171
Sharyn Blond Linens, 32, 36
Sheridan, Duffy, 68
Shreve Crump & Low, 83
Slesin, Suzanne, 210, 216
Sloane, Hans, 91
Smith, Kiki, 192
Society of the Cincinnati, 98, 101, 108

Solntsev, Fyodor, 182
Sotheby's, 15, 28, 64
Staffordshire salt-glazed stoneware, 46, 94, 205
Stamford, Connecticut, 15
Starburst Medallion, 192
Stately Homes of England, 256
Stately Homes of England Collection, 175, 187
    Chatsworth terriers, 187
Steinberg, Michael, 210
Steinway piano, 108
Stoneware, 46, 51, 94, 97, 102, 216, 219, 220, 228, 231
Sutherland, David, 152
Swan pattern, 88
Swansea, Wales, 83
Sylvanae pattern, 77
Syngchong, 118
Tessitura Toscana Telerie, 228
The Colonial Williamsburg Foundation, Williamsburg, Virginia, 132
The Reef, Palm Beach, Florida, 202, 226
Thos. Moser Furniture Company, 68, 73, 78
    Aria, 73
Tiffany & Co., 241
Tobacco Leaf pattern, 16, 31, 54, 196, 199, 210, 212, 216
Tobacco Leaf and Lace plates, 212
Toll, Barbara, 180, 182, 190, 192
Tom Mathieu and Company, 228
Tony Duquette, Inc., 192
Tony Duquette for Mottahedeh, 205, 256
Torquay, England, 83
Tsar Alexis, 182
Tsar Nicholas I, 182
United Nations Plaza, New York, New York, 15
United States Navy, 175
Urban Electric Company, 164
US Department of State, Washington, DC, 94
USS Nightingale, clipper ship, 83
Vallauris, France, 216, 219, 220
Varga Art Crystal, 40, 45
Venice, Italy, 134
Verditer Blue, 123
Virginia Blue pattern, 54, 132, 144
Vista Alegre, 36, 45
Vogue, 118
Warner Geoffrey, 219
Warren Platner for Knoll, 161
Washington, DC, 73
Washington, George, 20, 46, 93, 94, 97, 98, 101, 102, 106, 108, 132
Washington, Martha, 94, 102, 144
Waterdance, 87, 128
Wheatsheaf vase, 73
White House, Washington, DC, 18, 256
Wikinson, Hutton, 192, 226
WILLIAMSBURG, 132
Williamsburg wallpaper pattern, 40
Wilson, Dr. Fraser, 118
Wilson, Peter, 154, 226
Wilson, Woodrow, 20
Winterthur collection, 106, 117
Winterthur Elephant candlestick, 114
Winterthur Museum, Garden & Library, Winterthur, Delaware 15, 87, 93, 97, 98, 102, 108, 114, 117
    Chinese Parlor, 108
    Georgia Room, 117
    Lake Erie Hall, 114
    Phyfe Room, 106
Wong, Yuh-Shioh, 228
Wood, Captain William, 118
Woods, Richard, 223
Worcester Porcelain Manufactory, 132, 256
    "Duke of Gloucester" pattern, 132
World War II, 15
Wormley, Edward, 164
Worshipful Society of Apothecaries, London, England, 91
Wrong, Sebastian, 223
Wufu Bat, 64
Wufu bowl, 171
Wufu cachepot, 64, 171
Yarmouth, Maine, 83
Yongle period, 28
York, Maine, 78
Zafferano America, 182, 205
Zezé, 236, 241
Zsolnay Porcelain Manufactory, 77

CAPTIONS

COVER AND PAGE 254 The Chelsea Feather pattern in turquoise is a modern interpretation of a curvaceous Rococo shape, which originated in Worcester, England, in 1770. It is now paired with a lustrous-gold feathered edge and a bold, contemporary color.

ENDPAPERS Mottahedeh's most beloved patterns are hand-painted onto sugar cookies created by my daughters, Dana and Lauren. Each design is reduced to its essence and delicately rendered with a tiny brush. They are so beautiful it is hard to take a bite.

BACK OF FRONT ENDPAPERS The ornamental centerpiece or epergne, in the shape of a man holding a basket, has been in the Mottahedeh line for more than 40 years. It is hand-painted with gold accents and was the brainchild of Mildred Mottahedeh and Nelson Rockefeller, who had it created for a state dinner at the White House when he was vice president.

PAGE 1 The Presentation bowl is a new creation I designed looking forward to Mottahedeh's 100th anniversary. The interior of the bowl features a pomegranate, the Chinese symbol of fertility, abundance, and prosperity.

PAGE 2 This magnificent tin-glazed blue-and-white faience piece is a reproduction of a 17th-century original from Chatsworth House in England. The Dutch created this grand floral display piece to show off their prized tulips. Each section is filled with water to keep the flowers fresh.

PAGE 3 An Imperial Blue ginger jar and Blue Canton Shang vase sit on my reading table next to one of my favorite books.

PAGES 4–5 This life-like, hand-painted, striped tureen in the shape of a melon, with its stem and leaf under-platter, is sure to impress. The fashion for tureens in the form of animals, fruits, and vegetables was a well-known style in Italian faience in the late 1700s.

PAGE 6 Mottahedeh made many kinds of decorative items, and this is one of which we have no record. We believe it is of Italian origin, but there were a number of items produced in France as Mottahedeh had an office in Paris.

PAGES 8–9 The Chelsea lettuce tureens originated at the Chelsea Porcelain Manufactory in London, England, one of the earliest European factories.

Our tureen was found at Chillingham Castle in Northumberland, England, which was built in the 13th century and is on the Historic Houses list in England.

OPPOSITE CONTENTS This charming pattern has a contemporary vibrancy and versatility that belies its antique origins. Mottahedeh's Bargello dinnerware is adapted from English porcelain, from around 1810. Like the needlework for which it is named, it combines dashes of red, green, blue, yellow, orange, and magenta in a geometric patchwork enhanced by 22-karat gold lines. It is reminiscent of a contemporary Indonesian ikat.

OPPOSITE The Melon tureen and stand by Tony Duquette for Mottahedeh sits on a windowsill in the Nelson-Galt House in Colonial Williamsburg. The faience piece has been hand-painted with 22-karat matte gold accents.

BACK COVER A photographic montage of four of Mottahedeh's iconic patterns including, clockwise from top right: Chelsea Bird, Blue Canton, Tobacco Leaf, and Palma.

IG: @mottahedehchina

Mottahedeh's history is intimately tied to the history of America and Europe and the story of the development of porcelain. We are very proud of the prestigious affiliations the company has had over the years.

The Art Institute of Chicago
Colonial Williamsburg
Dallas Museum of Art
Decatur House
Department of State
Hillwood Estate, Museum & Gardens
Historic Charleston Foundation
Historic Deerfield
Historic Natchez Foundation
Monticello
Mount Vernon
Musée des Arts Décoratifs
Passion for Maps
Smithsonian Institution
Stately Homes of England
The Jewish Museum
The John and Carolyn Grossman Collection
The Metropolitan Museum of Art
National Trust for Historic Preservation
The Nelson A. Rockefeller Collection
The Royal Pavilion & Garden
Tony Duquette
Winterthur Museum, Garden & Library

PHOTOGRAPHY CREDITS

ANTOINE BOOTZ cover, back cover, front and back endpapers, 1, 2, 4–5, 6, 17–47, 50–59, 66–82, 84–87, 90–92, top left and right, bottom left, 95–117, 133–141, 143–213, 217–243, 255, and opposite. PATRICK BRICKMAN 92, bottom right, 119, 120–121, 122, 123, 124, 125, 126–127, 128, 129, 130, 131. WENDY KVALHEIM 61, 62–63, 72. MATTHEW MEAD PHOTOGRAPHY 3, 10, 65. TOM NEUENSCHWANDER PHOTOGRAPHY 8–9, 48–49, 83, 88–89. ANNIE SCHLECTER 142. SUZANNE SLESIN 214–215. WHITE LIGHT PHOTOGRAPHY 14.
Every effort has been made to locate the holders of copyright; any omissions will be corrected in future printings.

PUBLISHER / EDITORIAL DIRECTOR Suzanne Slesin
CREATIVE DIRECTOR Frederico Farina
EDITORIAL ASSISTANT Julian Cosma
COPY EDITOR Valerie Saint-Rossy
ISBN 978-1-938461-60-6 / LIBRARY OF CONGRESS 2023917954
PRINTED IN SPAIN / FIRST EDITION

Splendid Settings: 100 years of Mottahedeh Design © 2024 Wendy Kvalheim. All rights reserved under international copyright conventions. No part of this book or any of its content may be reproduced, utilized or transmitted in any form or by any means, electronic or mechanical, including photocopying, recording or by any information storage and retrieval system, or otherwise, without permission in writing from the publisher. Please contact info@pointedleafpress.com or visit pointedleafpress.com to place an order or for all other inquiries. Pointed Leaf Press, LLC, 136 Baxter Street, Suite 1C, New York, New York, 10013.